JANE'S POCKET BOOK OF LIGHT AIRCRAFT

JANE'S POCKET BOOK OF LIGHT AIRCRAFT

Compiled by MICHAEL J. H. TAYLOR and KENNETH MUNSON
Edited by JOHN W. R. TAYLOR, FRHistS, AFRAeS, FSLAET

COLLIER BOOKS
A Division of Macmillan Publishing Co., Inc.
New York

Macmillan Publishing Co., Inc.
866 Third Avenue, New York, N.Y. 10022
Collier Macmillan Canada, Ltd.
Library of Congress Catalog Card Number: 74-10313

First Collier Books Edition 1976
Second Printing 1977

Printed in the United States of America

FOREWORD

This fourth volume in the series of *Jane's* Pocket Books of Major Aircraft deals with what the US industry calls "General Aviation" types. As a class, they are the smallest and least powerful products of the world aerospace industry. They are also, by far, the most numerous, and closest to the kind of flying machines of which the pioneers dreamed for countless centuries.

In the eyes of the man and woman by the television screen, combat aircraft will always be flown by a race of dedicated supermen; and airlines offer air travel rather than flying. Not until size and power are scaled down to produce the designs illustrated in this book are the grim purposes of war and the economic dictates of airline operations replaced by thoughts of pure pleasure, competition, and attention to the personal, everyday crises in which the lives of our neighbours can be saved by speedy transport to hospital, and the lives of our crops can be saved by the efficient application of chemicals. The two largest air forces in the world each possess about 14 000 aircraft, for first-line, transport and training duties. The International Civil Aviation Organisation, counting most of the world's aircraft-operating nations among its 124 member states, reported a total of 7 454 commercial transport aircraft in worldwide service at the last census. By comparison, the USA alone claimed a total of 131 870 "active" civil aircraft when statistics were last compiled in November 1973, of which the vast majority were clearly in the categories covered in this book.

According to the Aerospace Industries Association of America, the number of utility and executive aircraft built in the USA in 1973 was expected to total approximately 13 600, compared with only 300 turbine-powered airliners. The Soviet Union cannot match such production, with only 7 000 of its standard Yak-18s built to date; but flying for fun is encouraged there too. Membership of its technical sports organisation, DOSAAF, costs a mere 1.5 roubles (less than £1) a year for students or 3 roubles for working adults, after which all expenses – aircraft, tuition, fuel and airfield charges – are met by DOSAAF. The number of aircraft engaged on agricultural flying in the Soviet Union can be gauged from the fact that 1 250 million acres of arable land are being treated with fertilisers and herbicides by spraying and dusting aircraft during the period of the current five-year plan.

Confronted with such statistics, one gains a fresh appreciation of the importance of these seemingly less spectacular brethren of the Jumbos and supersonic fighters found in the earlier Pocket Books. As always, the information given for each type is that which will best aid its identification, without extraneous facts about its history and structure. Anyone who wants that much detail can find it in the million and a half words of each annual edition of *Jane's All the World's Aircraft*. The Pocket Books are intended as easy-to-handle day-to-day working aids for people whose job or delight it is to recognise aircraft.

JOHN W. R. TAYLOR

First flights 1963 / 1967 (?)

Single-seat agricultural aircraft

AAMSA / AERO COMMANDER SPARROW COMMANDER and QUAIL COMMANDER (Mexico)

Data: Sparrow Commander
Power plant: One Lycoming O-540-B2B5 six-cylinder piston engine (235 hp)
Wing span: 34 ft 9 in (10.59 m)
Length overall: 23 ft 6 in (7.16 m)
Weight empty: 1 600 lb (726 kg)
Max payload: 1 400 lb (635 kg)
Max T-O weight (Agricultural): 3 400 lb (1 542 kg)
Max cruising speed (75% power) at 3 000 lb (1 360 kg) AUW: 91 knots (105 mph; 169 km/h)
Max rate of climb at S/L (Agricultural): 650 ft (198 m)/min
Service ceiling (Agricultural): 14 000 ft (4 265 m)
Range at max cruising speed (Agricultural): 260 nm (300 miles; 483 km)
Accommodation: Single seat. Capacity of standard hopper 22.5 cu ft (0.64 m³) or 170 gallons (643 litres)
Variants: Both types available with liquid spray or dust dispersal gear, or with a quick-change combination dust or spray unit; Quail Commander differs only in having a 290 hp Lycoming IO-540-G1C5 fuel-injection engine and a 210 US gallon (795 litre) capacity hopper. In production (both)

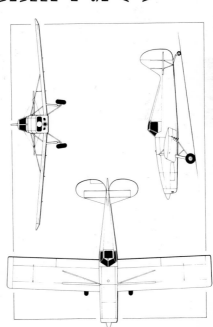

Photo and Drawing: Quail Commander

7

AERO-3 (Yugoslavia)

First flight 1957(?)

Two-seat primary trainer

Power plant: One Lycoming O-435-A six-cylinder piston engine (185 hp)
Wing span: 34 ft 5½ in (10.50 m)
Length overall: 28 ft 1¾ in (8.58 m)
Max T-O weight: 2 641 lb (1 198 kg)
Max cruising speed at 2 950 ft (900 m): 97 knots (112 mph; 180 km/h)
Service ceiling: 14 100 ft (4 300 m)
Range: 366 nm (422 miles; 680 km)
Accommodation: Seating for two persons in tandem. Dual controls
Variants: Standard version, as described above, equipped for either military or civil use

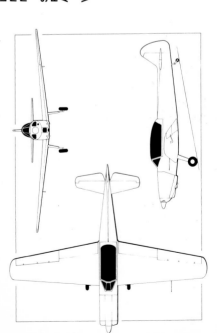

9

AERO BOERO 95, 115 and 180 (Argentine Republic)

First flights 1959 / 1967(?)

Three-seat light aircraft

Length overall: 23 ft 10¼ in (7.273 m)
Weight empty, equipped: 1 212 lb (550 kg)
Max T-O weight: 1 860 lb (844 kg)
Max cruising speed at S/L: 114 knots (131 mph; 211 km/h)
Max rate of climb at S/L: 1 180 ft (360 m)/min
Service ceiling: 22 000 ft (6 700 m)
Range with max fuel: 429 nm (495 miles; 800 km)
Accommodation: Pilot and two passengers.

Variants:

AB 95 Standard. Initial three-seat production version: 95 hp Continental C90, 34 ft 2¼ in (10.42 m) span

AB 95A De Lujo. 100 hp Continental O-200-A

AB 95A Fumigador. Agricultural version of AB 95A:

AB 95B. 150 hp engine

AB 95/115. Similar to AB 95B, but 115 hp Lycoming O-235-C2A, mainwheel fairings, more streamlined cowling

AB 115 BS. Current version (first flight 1973), developed from AB 95/115: 35 ft 2 in (10.72 m) span, sweptback fin and rudder, extra fuel. In production

AB 180. Initial four-seat version: 180 hp Lycoming O-360-A1A, 35 ft 1 in (10.70 m) span. Also produced as three-seater with 34 ft 2¼ in (10.42 m) span

AB 180 RV. Current three-seat standard version (first flight 1972) 35 ft 2 in (10.72 m) span, recontoured fuselage, sweptback fin and rudder, extra fuel. In production

AB 180 RVR. As above with glider hook. In production.

AB 180 Condor. High-altitude version of AB 180 RV: modified wingtips, optional turbocharger. Pilot and passenger or 220 lb (100 kg) under fuselage cargo pack.

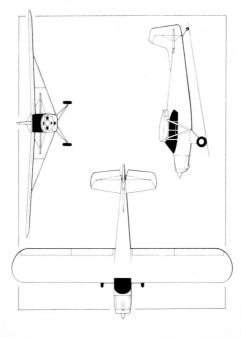

Photo: AB 180 Condor
Drawing: AB 95
Data: AB 180 RV
Power plant: One Lycoming O-360-A1A four-cylinder piston engine (180 hp)
Wing span: 35 ft 2 in (10.72 m)

11

AERO BOERO 210/260 (Argentine Republic)

Data: AB 210
Power plant: One Continental IO-360 six-cylinder piston engine (210 hp).
Wing span: 35 ft 2 in (10.72 m)
Length overall: 24 ft 3¾ in (7.40 m)
Cabin:
  Max length: 5 ft 8 in (1.73 m)
  Max width: 3 ft 1 in (0.94 m)
  Max height: 3 ft 11 in (1.19 m)
  Volume: 52 cu ft (1.50 m³)
Weight empty, equipped: 1 477 lb (670 kg)
Max T-O weight: 2 425 lb (1 100 kg)
Max cruising speed at 5 900 ft (1 800 m), estimated: 122 knots (140 mph; 225 km/h)
Max rate of climb at S/L, estimated: 1 180 ft (360 m)/min
Service ceiling, estimated: 19 675 ft (6 000 m)
Range with max fuel, estimated: 429 nm (495 miles; 800 km)
Accommodation: Pilot and three passengers. All passenger seats removable
Variants: Prototype AB 210 only: as described above. Proposed development as Aero Boero 260, after being fitted with 260 hp Lycoming O-540 engine

First flight 1971

Four-seat light aircraft

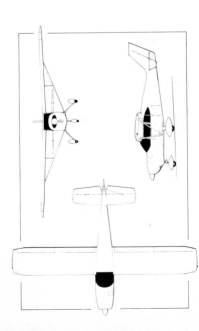

Photo: AB 210

13

First flight 1972

Single-seat agricultural aircraft

AERO BOERO AG.260 (Argentine Republic)

Data: Prototype

Power plant: One Lycoming O-540 six-cylinder piston engine (260 hp)

Wing span: 35 ft 9¼ in (10.90 m)

Length overall (tail up): 24 ft 5¼ in (7.45 m)

Weight empty: 1 587 lb (720 kg)

Max T-O weight: 2 976 lb (1 350 kg)

Max cruising speed at S/L: 109 knots (125 mph; 201 km/h)

Max rate of climb at S/L: 1 345 ft (410 m)/min

Service ceiling: 21 000 ft (6 400 m)

Range with max fuel: 377 nm (435 miles; 700 km)

Accommodation: Single seat. Utility compartment on port side, aft of cabin

Equipment: Non-corrosive glassfibre tank installed forward of cockpit, with capacity of 110 Imp gallons (500 litres) of liquid or 1 102 lb (500 kg) of dry chemical

Variants: Prototype only, as described above

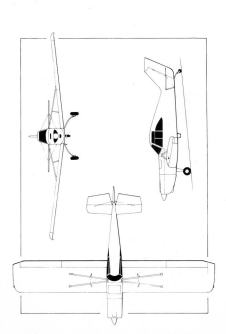

AERONCA 15AC SEDAN (USA)

First flight 1947

Four-seat light aircraft

Power plant: One Continental C145 six-cylinder piston engine (145 hp)
Wing span: 37 ft 6 in (11.43 m)
Length overall: 25 ft 3 in (7.70 m)
Weight empty: 1 150 lb (522 kg)
Max T-O weight: 2 050 lb (930 kg)
Max cruising speed (75% power) at S/L: 99 knots (114 mph; 183 km/h)
Rate of climb at S/L: 800 ft (245 m)/min
Service ceiling: 12 400 ft (3 780 m)
Normal range: 396 nm (456 miles; 734 km)
Accommodation: Seating for four persons. Dual controls. Rear seat removable. Baggage compartment aft of cabin with capacity of 120 lb (54.4 kg)
Variants: Standard version, as described above. Some aircraft have 165 hp Franklin 6A40-165-B3 engine; some built as **S15AC** twin-float seaplanes

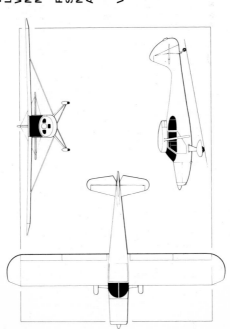

AEROSPACE (VICTA / AESL) AIRTOURER series (New Zealand)

First flight 1959

Two-seat light aircraft

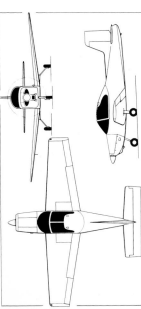

Photo: Airtourer T4
Drawing: Airtourer T2

Data: Airtourer T4
Power plant: One Lycoming O-320-E2A four-cylinder piston engine (150 hp)
Wing span: 26 ft 0 in (7.92 m)
Length overall: 21 ft 5⅞ in (6.55 m)

Cabin:
Length: 5 ft 8 in (1.73 m)
Max width: 3 ft 6 in (1.07 m)
Max height: 4 ft 2 in (1.27 m)
Baggage space: 8 cu ft (0.23 m³)
Weight empty, equipped: 1 165 lb (528 kg)
Max T-O weight (Normal): 1 750 lb (793 kg)
Max cruising speed at 4 000 ft (1 220 m): 122 knots (140 mph; 225 km/h)
Max rate of climb at S/L: 980 ft (299 m)/min
Service ceiling: 15 500 ft (4 725 m)
Range with max fuel, no allowances: 542 nm (625 miles; 1 005 km)
Accommodation: Two seats side by side. Dual controls. Baggage compartment aft of seats with capacity of 100 lb (45 kg)
Variants:
Airtourer 100. Initial production version: 100 hp Continental O-200-A
Airtourer T2 (originally Airtourer 115). 115 hp Lycoming O-235-C2A, fixed-pitch propeller
Airtourer T3. As T2 except 130 hp Rolls-Royce Continental O-240-A, fixed-pitch propeller. In production
Airtourer T4. As T2 except 150 hp Lycoming O-320-E2A, fixed-pitch propeller, increased AUW. In production
Airtourer T5. As T4 except 150 hp Lycoming O-320-E1A, constant-speed propeller, needle-type spinner. In production
Airtourer T6/12. As T5 but increased AUW, 12V electrical system. In production
Airtourer T6/24. As T6/12 but 24V electrical system. In production

AEROSPACE (AIR PARTS / FLETCHER) FU-24 series (New Zealand)

First flight 1954

Agricultural and utility passenger / cargo aircraft

Weight empty, equipped: 2 616 lb (1 186 kg)
Max payload (agricultural): 2 320 lb (1 052 kg)
Normal max T-O weight: 4 860 lb (2 204 kg)
Special T-O weight: 5 430 lb (2 463 kg)
Max cruising speed: 106 knots (122 mph; 196 km/h)
Max rate of climb at S/L: 630 ft (192 m)/min
Service ceiling: 16 000 ft (4 875 m)
Range with max fuel: 382 nm (440 miles; 708 km)

Accommodation: Agricultural version seats pilot and 1 passenger. Utility version seats pilot and 5 passengers in FU-24, in FU-24-950, or freight. Dual controls optional

Agricultural equipment: Variety of equipment available for top-dressing, seeding and low- and high-volume spraying

Variants:

FU-24. Original Fletcher-built agricultural and 5-seat utility version: 260 hp Continental IO-470-D

FU-24A. Fletcher-developed 6-seat cargo version

FU-24. Standard NZ-built agricultural version: 300 hp Rolls-Royce Continental IO-520-F. Also version with 4/5 seats or 1 680 lb cargo

FU-24A. In production.

FU-24-950. Agricultural version (400 hp Lycoming), as described. Also 8-seat utility version. In production.

Air Parts Fletcher 1060. Enlarged development of FU-24 (first flight 1967): 500 shp UACL PT6A-20 turboprop

Air Parts Fletcher 1160. Basically as 1060 but with 530 shp AiResearch TPE 331

Aerospace Fletcher 1284. Current turboprop version (first flight 1970): 665 shp AiResearch TPE 331-1-101 Built in agricultural or 9-passenger utility versions

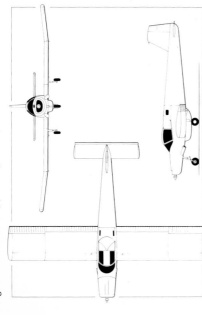

Photo and Drawing: FU-24 (300 hp)

Data: FU-24-950
Power plant: One Lycoming IO-720-A1A eight-cylinder piston engine (400 hp)
Wing span: 42 ft 0 in (12.81 m)
Length overall: 32 ft 9 in (9.98 m)
Cabin: Length: 10 ft 5 in (3.18 m). Max width: 4 ft 0 in (1.22 m)

21

AÉROSPATIALE ALOUETTE II (France)

First flight 1955

Five-seat general-purpose helicopter

Data: SA 318C Alouette II Astazou

Power plant: One Turboméca Astazou IIA turboshaft engine (530 shp, derated to 360 shp)

Main rotor diameter: 33 ft 5⅝ in (10.20 m)

Fuselage length, tail rotor turning: 31 ft 11¾ in (9.75 m)

Weight empty: 1 961 lb (890 kg)

Max T-O weight: 3 630 lb (1 650 kg)

Max cruising speed at S/L: 97 knots (112 mph; 180 km/h)

Max rate of climb at S/L: 1 300 ft (396 m)/min

Service ceiling: 10 800 ft (3 300 m)

Range with max fuel at S/L: 388 nm (447 miles; 720 km)

Range with 1 058 lb (480 kg) payload: 161 nm (186 miles; 300 km)

Accommodation: Pilot and passenger side by side in forward part of cabin and three passengers behind. Can be adapted, with a raised skid gear, for flying crane (payload 1 322 lb; 600 kg), rescue (hoist capacity 265 lb; 120 kg), ambulance (two stretchers and a medical attendant), agricultural or photographic duties

Variants:

SE 313 Alouette II Artouste. Original version, with 530 shp (derated to 360 shp) Turboméca Artouste IIC6 turboshaft. Production (923) completed

SA 318 Alouette II Astazou. Current production version, as described above

SA 315 Lama. Reinforced Alouette II airframe combined with power plant and rotor system of Alouette III. In production

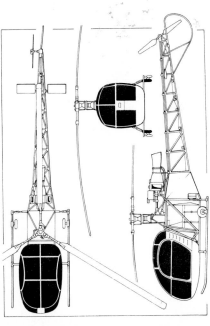

Photo: SE 313 Alouette II
Drawing: SA 318 Alouette II Astazou

AÉROSPATIALE ALOUETTE III (France)

First flight 1959

Seven-seat general-purpose helicopter

Data: SA 316B

Power plant: One Turboméca Artouste IIIB turboshaft engine (870 shp, derated to 570 shp)

Main rotor diameter: 36 ft 1¾ in (11.02 m)

Length overall, rotors turning: 42 ft 1½ in (12.84 m)

Weight empty: 2 474 lb (1 122 kg)

Max T-O weight: 4 850 lb (2 200 kg)

Max cruising speed at S/L: 100 knots (115 mph: 185 km/h)

Max rate of climb at S/L: 885 ft (270 m)/min

Service ceiling: 13 125 ft (4 000 m)

Range with max fuel at S/L: 258 nm (298 miles: 480 km)

Accommodation: Normal accommodation for pilot and six passengers. Two baggage holds in centre-section. Provision for carrying two stretchers athwartships at rear of cabin, and two other persons, in addition to the pilot. All passenger seats removable to enable freight to be carried. Provision for external sling for loads of up to 1 650 lb (750 kg). Dual controls optional

Variants:

SA 316B Alouette III (originally SE 3160). Standard major production version, as described above

SA 319 Alouette III Astazou. Similar to SA 316B but with 870 shp (derated to 600 shp) Turboméca Astazou XIV. In production

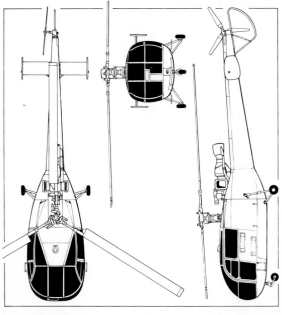

Photo and Drawing: SA 316B Alouette III

AÉROSPATIALE/WESTLAND SA 341 GAZELLE (France)

First flight 1967

Five-seat light utility helicopter

Data: SA 341G

Power plant: One Turboméca Astazou IIIA turboshaft engine (590 shp)

Main rotor diameter: 34 ft 5½ in (10.50 m)

Length of fuselage: 31 ft 3³⁄₁₆ in (9.53 m)

Cabin:

Length: 7 ft 2⁹⁄₁₆ in (2.20 m)
Max width: 4 ft 4 in (1.32 m)
Max height: 3 ft 11⅝ in (1.21 m)
Volume: 63.7 cu ft (1.80 m³)

Baggage hold volume: 15.9 cu ft (0.45 m³)

Weight empty: 2 022 lb (917 kg)

Max T-O weight: 3 970 lb (1 800 kg)

Max cruising speed at S/L: 142 knots (164 mph; 264 km/h)

Max rate of climb at S/L: 1 770 ft (540 m)/min

Service ceiling: 16 400 ft (5 000 m)

Range at S/L with max fuel: 361 nm (416 miles; 670 km)

Range with crew of 1 and 1 102 lb (500 kg) payload: 193.5 nm (223 miles; 360 km)

Accommodation: Crew of one or two and seating for three passengers on bench seat to rear of cabin. The bench seat can be folded away to leave a completely flat cargo floor. Baggage compartment at rear of cabin. Dual controls optional

Equipment: A variety of operational equipment can be fitted, according to role, including a 1 322 lb (600 kg) cargo sling, 264 lb (120 kg) rescue hoist, stretcher, or photographic and survey equipment

Civil variants: SA 341G, as described above. In production

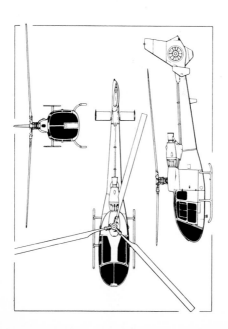

AEROSTAR and MOONEY M-20 series (USA)

Cabin: Length: 8 ft 8 in (2.64 m)
  Max width: 3 ft 4½ in (1.04 m)
  Max height: 3 ft 8½ in (1.13 m)

Baggage compartment: 13.5 cu ft (0.38 m³)
Weight empty: 1 525 lb (691 kg)
Max T-O weight: 2 575 lb (1 168 kg)
Max level speed at S/L: 153 knots (176 mph; 283 km/h)
Max rate of climb at S/L: 1 000 ft (305 m)/min
Service ceiling: 19 500 ft (5 743 m)
Range, with allowances for taxi, climb and 45 min reserves: 869 nm (1 001 miles; 1 610 km)
Accommodation: Four seats in pairs. Dual controls. Starboard front and rear seats removable for freight stowage. Compartment for 120 lb baggage behind cabin
Equipment: Choice of six different factory-installed electronics packages and two optional equipment packages

Variants:

Mooney M-20. 150 hp Lycoming O-320 engine

Mooney M-20A. Higher-powered M-20: 180 hp Lycoming O-360-A engine

Aerostar Ranger (originally Mooney M-20C Mk 21).

Mooney M-20D Master. Simplified M-20C: non-retractable landing gear, less comprehensive equipment

Aerostar Chaparral (originally Mooney M-20E Super-21). Similar to Ranger but 200 hp Lycoming IO-360-A1A

Aerostar (originally Mooney M-20F) Executive. Similar to Ranger but 200 hp Lycoming IO-360-A1A engine, longer fuselage and additional windows.

Mooney M-20G Statesman. Similar to Ranger, but with longer fuselage and extra cabin windows of Executive

First flight 1953

Four-seat light aircraft

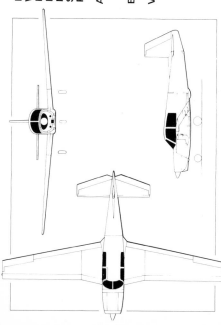

Photo and Drawing: Ranger.
Data: Aerostar Ranger
Power plant: One Lycoming O-360-A1D four-cylinder piston engine (180 hp)
Wing span: 35 ft 0 in (10.67 m)
Length overall: 24 ft 1 in (7.34 m)

AEROTEC UIRAPURU (Brazil)

First flight 1965

Two-seat light aircraft

Power plant: One Lycoming O-320-B2B four-cylinder piston engine (160 hp)
Wing span: 27 ft 10¾ in (8.50 m)
Length overall: 21 ft 8 in (6.60 m)
Weight empty: 1 191 lb (540 kg)
Max T-O weight: 1 825 lb (840 kg)
Max cruising speed at 5 000 ft (1 525 m): 100 knots (115 mph; 185 km/h)
Max rate of climb at S/L: 787 ft (240 m)/min
Service ceiling: 14 760 ft (4 500 m)
Max range: 700 nm (805 miles; 1 300 km)
Max endurance: 6 hr 30 min
Accommodation: Two seats side by side. Dual controls. Baggage compartment, capacity 66 lb (30 kg), aft of seats
Civil variants: Initial version, as described above. In production

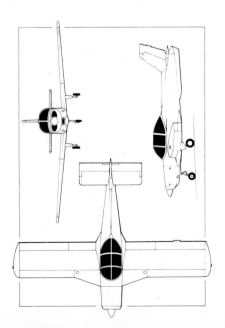

AISA I-11B (Spain)

First flight 1950

Two-seat light aircraft

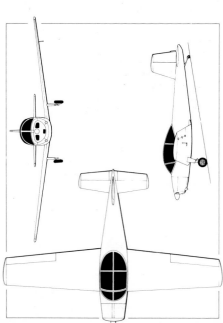

Power plant: One Continental C90-12F four-cylinder piston engine (90 hp)
Wing span: 30 ft 7 in (9.34 m)
Length overall: 21 ft 3 in (6.47 m)
Weight empty: 926 lb (421 kg)
Normal T-O weight: 1 417 lb (644 kg)
Max permissible weight (semi-aerobatic): 1 474 lb (670 kg)
Cruising speed at normal T-O weight: 96 knots (110 mph; 177 km/h)
Max rate of climb at S/L at normal T-O weight: 726 ft (200 m)/min
Service ceiling at normal T-O weight: 15 415 ft (4 700 m)
Range with max fuel at normal T-O weight: 349 nm (403 miles; 650 km)
Accommodation: Two seats side by side, with dual controls. Baggage space aft of seats
Civil variants: Some aircraft powered by 93 hp ENMA Flecha engine

ANAHUAC TAURO 300 (BULL) (Mexico)

Single-seat agricultural aircraft

Data: Standard version
Power plant: One Jacobs R-755-A2M1 seven-cylinder piston engine (300 hp)
Wing span: 37 ft 6½ in (11.44 m)
Length overall: 26 ft 11¼ in (8.21 m)
Cabin:
  Max length: 3 ft 8 in (1.12 m)
  Max width: 2 ft 10 in (0.86 m)
  Max height: 4 ft 3 in (1.295 m)
Weight empty: 1 973 lb (895 kg)
Max T-O weight: 3 542 lb (1 606 kg)
Max cruising speed at S/L: 78 knots (90 mph; 145 km/h)
Max rate of climb at S/L: 500 ft (152 m)/min
Service ceiling: 14 000 ft (4 250 m)
Range with max fuel: 202 nm (233 miles; 375 km)
Accommodation: Single seat
Equipment: Chemical hopper in fuselage, forward of cockpit at CG position, capacity 230 US gallons (191 Imp gallons; 870 litres) of liquid or 1 764 lb (800 kg) of dry chemical. Transland dispersal equipment
Variants: Available optionally with 350 hp Jacobs R-755-SM engine and fixed-pitch or constant-speed propeller. In production

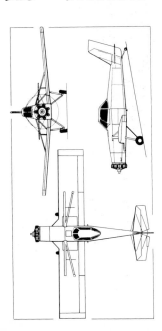

AUSTER series / BEAGLE D series (UK)

First flights 1939 / 1960

Two- to four-seat light aircraft

Data: D.5 / 180 Husky

Power plant: One Lycoming O-360-A2A four-cylinder piston engine (180 hp)

Wing span: 36 ft 0 in (10.97 m)

Length overall: 22 ft 2 in (6.76 m)

Weight empty, equipped: 1 420 lb (645 kg)

Max T-O weight: 2 400 lb (1 088 kg)

Max cruising speed: 96 knots (110 mph; 177 km/h)

Max rate of climb at S/L: 800 ft (245 m)/min

Service ceiling: 14 500 ft (4 420 m)

Max range, no reserves: 503 nm (580 miles; 930 km)

Accommodation: Pilot and three passengers, in pairs.

Equipment: Optional equipment includes blind-flying instrumentation, equipment for crop-spraying, cable-laying, aerial photography, glider towing and stretcher carrying

Civil variants:

Taylorcraft Plus C, Taylorcraft Plus D (8 built), **Auster 2** (2 built), **Model F Auster 3** (470 built), **Model G Auster 4** (254 built), **Model J Auster 5** (790 built; version with rear fuselage of Autocar known as Alpha 5), **Auster 6A Tugmaster, Auster J/1 Autocrat** (420 built), **Auster J/1B Aiglet, Auster J/1N Alpha, Auster J/1U Workmaster, Auster J/2 Arrow** (44 built; 1 converted to J/3 Atom), **Auster J/4** (26 built), **Auster J/5** (50 built), **Auster J/5B Autocar** (approx 100 built), **Auster J/5F Aiglet Trainer** (variants include J/5K and J/5L, approx 70 built), **Auster J/5G Autocar** (approx 80 built), **Auster J/5P Autocar** (approx 20 built), **Auster J/5R Alpine** (variant J/5Q), **Auster J/8L Aiglet Trainer** (1 conversion of J/5K), **Beagle-Auster D.4/108, Beagle D.5/160** and **D.5/180 Husky, Beagle-Auster D.6/180** (4 built) and **A.61 Terrier** (60 converted from military AOP 6)

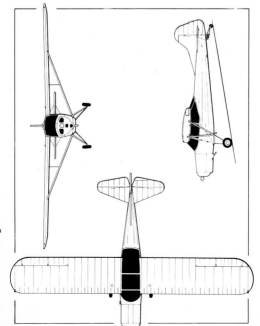

Photo: A.61 Terrier
Drawing: D.5/180 Husky

BEAGLE A.109 AIREDALE (UK)

First flight 1961

Four-seat light aircraft

Data: A.109
Power plant: One Lycoming O-360-A1A four-cylinder piston engine (180 hp)
Wing span: 36 ft 4 in (11.07 m)
Length overall: 26 ft 4 in (8.02 m)
Cabin:
 Length: 6 ft 9 in (2.06 m)
 Max width: 3 ft 4 in (1.02 m)
 Max height: 3 ft 9 in (1.14 m)
Baggage compartment: 5 cu ft (0.14 m³)
Weight empty, equipped: 1 700 lb (771 kg)
Max T-O weight: 2 750 lb (1 247 kg)
Max cruising speed at 6 000 ft (1 830 m): 116 knots (133 mph, 214 km/h)
Max rate of climb at S/L: 650 ft (198 m)/min
Service ceiling: 12 000 ft (3 660 m)
Max range with 660 lb (300 kg) payload and 50 Imp gallons (227 litres) fuel, no reserve: 720 nm (830 miles; 1 337 km)
Accommodation: Seating for four persons, in pairs. Dual steering-wheel controls standard. Space for briefcases and small objects in rear of cabin, in addition to baggage compartment
Variants:
 Standard **A.109**, as described above; experimental **A.111**, with 175 hp Continental GO-300 engine

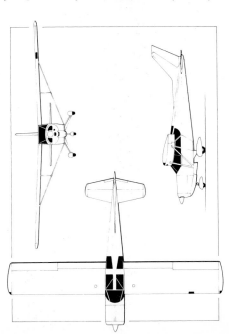

39

BEAGLE B.121 PUP (UK)

First flight 1967

Two / three-seat light aircraft

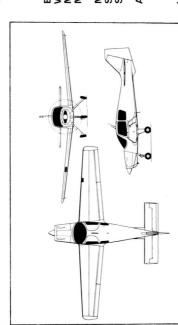

Photo: Pup-150
Drawing: Pup-100
Data: Pup-150 (B.121 Series 2)
Power plant: One Lycoming O-320-A2B four-cylinder piston engine (150 hp)

Wing span: 31 ft 0 in (9.45 m)
Length overall: 23 ft 2 in (7.06 m)
Cabin:

Length: 6 ft 6 in (1.98 m)
Max width: 3 ft 9 in (1.14 m)
Max height: 3 ft 6 in (1.07 m)
Volume: 85 cu ft (2.41 m³)

Baggage space: 15 cu ft (0.42 m³)
Weight empty, equipped: 1 090 lb (494 kg)
Max T-O weight: 1 925 lb (873 kg)
Max cruising speed (75% power) at 7 500 ft (2 290 m): 114 knots (131 mph; 211 km/h)
Max rate of climb at S/L: 800 ft (244 m)/min
Service ceiling: 14 700 ft (4 480 m)
Still-air range with optional fuel: 549 nm (633 miles; 1 020 km)

Accommodation: Standard seating for two persons, with optional third seat to rear on starboard side for one adult passenger or occasional seats for two children. Dual controls standard. Baggage compartment aft of seats

Variants:

Pup-100 (B.121 Series 1). Two-seat fully-aerobatic version: 100 hp Rolls-Royce Continental O-200-A engine
Pup-150 (B.121 Series 2). Similar to Pup-100 but more powerful engine and increased accommodation, as described above, and optional fuel increase from 24 to 34 Imp gallons (109 to 155 litres)
Pup-160 (B.121 Series 3). Designation of 6 aircraft for an Iranian customer, with "2 + 2" seating, 160 hp Lycoming O-320-D2C engine, and standard fuel capacity of 36 Imp gallons (164 litres) with no optional increase

41

BEAGLE B.206 (UK)

First flight 1961

Twin-engined light business transport

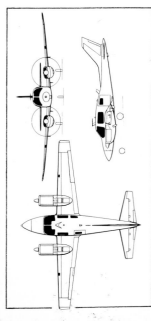

Photo: B.206 Series II

Data: B.206 Series II (B.206-S)

Power plant: Two Rolls-Royce Continental GTSIO-520-C six-cylinder turbocharged piston engines (each 340 hp)

Wing span: 45 ft 9½ in (13.96 m)

Length overall: 33 ft 8 in (10.26 m)

Cabin:

Length: 11 ft 11 in (3.63 m)
Max width: 5 ft 2 in (1.57 m)
Max height: 4 ft 4 in (1.32 m)
Volume: 196.5 cu ft (5.56 m³)

Baggage compartment (aft of cabin): 21 cu ft (0.59 m³)

Weight empty: 4 800 lb (2 177 kg)

Max T-O weight: 7 499 lb (3 401 kg)

Max cruising speed (75% power) at 8 000 ft (2 440 m), at 7 000 lb (3 175 kg) AUW: 189 knots (218 mph; 351 km/h)

Max rate of climb at S/L at max T-O weight: 1 340 ft (408 m)/min

Service ceiling at 7 000 lb (3 175 kg) AUW: 27 100 ft (8 260 m)

Range with max fuel, no allowances, at max T-O weight: 1 389 nm (1 600 miles; 2 570 km)

Accommodation: Standard seating for five/eight persons. Air survey version can accommodate single or dual cameras in cabin floor. Ambulance version carries pilot, two stretchers and a medical attendant. Utilisation in a cargo-carrying role is accomplished by removal of rear seats, providing 44 sq ft (4.09 m²) of floor area. Baggage compartment aft of cabin

Variants:

B.206 Series I (B.206C). Initial commercial production version: 310 hp Rolls-Royce Continental GIO-470-A non-turbocharged engines. Early aircraft have overwing cabin door, later aircraft a passenger/cargo door aft of wings

B.206 Series II (B.206-S). Development of Series I, as described above, with turbocharged engines. Later production aircraft have extended cabin, additional rear window each side, and large passenger/cargo door at rear on port side

B.206 Series III. Developed version, seating 10 passengers, with dorsal and ventral fins, small tabs on main fin, extended tailplane trailing-edge. Prototype only

BEECHCRAFT BARON series (USA)

First flight 1960

Light business and general-purpose transport

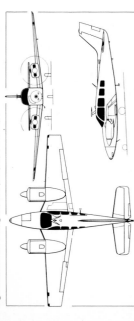

Photo: B55 Baron
Drawing: Baron 58
Data: Baron 58
Power plant: Two Continental IO-520-C six-cylinder piston engines (each 285 hp)
Wing span: 37 ft 10 in (11.53 m)
Length overall: 29 ft 10 in (9.09 m)
Cabin, including rear baggage area:
Length: 12 ft 10 in (3.91 m), Max width: 3 ft 6 in (1.07 m)
Max height: 4 ft 2 in (1.27 m). Volume: 135.9 cu ft (3.85 m³)
Baggage compartments:
fwd: 18 cu ft (0.51 m³), rear: 37 cu ft (1.05 m³)
Extended rear baggage compartment: 10 cu ft (0.28 m³)
Weight empty, equipped: 3 268 lb (1 482 kg)

Max T-O weight: 5 400 lb (2 449 kg)
Max cruising speed (75% power) at 7 000 ft (2 135 m):
200 knots (230 mph; 370 km/h)
Max rate of climb at S/L: 1 694 ft (516 m)/min
Service ceiling: 17 800 ft (5 425 m)
Range (65% power) at 11 000 ft (3 355 m) with optional fuel; allowance for warm-up, taxi, take-off and climb to altitude with 45 min fuel reserve: 1 052 nm (1 212 miles; 1 950 km)

Accommodation: Standard seating for four persons, in pairs. Folding fifth and sixth seats optional. Forward baggage compartment capacity 300 lb (136 kg); rear baggage compartment 400 lb (181 kg); space in extended rear compartment for 120 lb (54 kg) of baggage. Passenger seats removable for cargo carrying

Variants:

Model 95-55. 1960 four/five-seat development of earlier Travel Air: 260 hp Continental IO-470-L engines, sweptback fin and rudder

A55. 1962 version: optional sixth seat

B55. 1964 version: longer nose, higher operating weights. In production

C55. 1964 version: similar to B55 but slightly heavier and with 285 hp Continental IO-520-C engines. Updated versions **D55** (1968), **E55** (1970) in production (E55).

Turbo Baron. 1968 version: 380 hp Lycoming TIO-541-C turbocharged engines

Baron 58. 1970 version, as described above. Similar to E55 but longer front fuselage, extra cabin windows, passenger/cargo double doors. In production

45

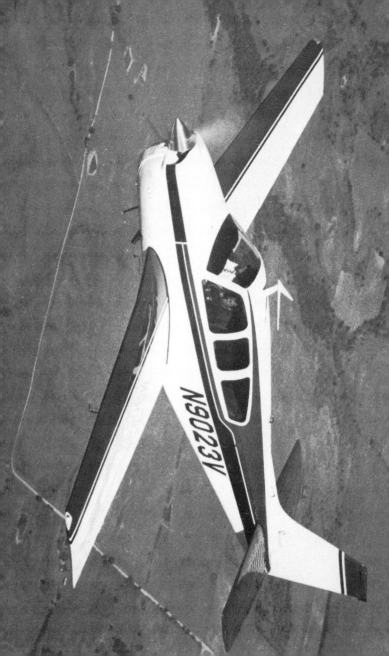

BEECHCRAFT MODELS 33 and 36 BONANZA (conventional tail) (USA)

First flight 1959

Four- to six-seat light aircraft

Weight empty, equipped: 2 096 lb (951 kg)
Max T-O weight: 3 600 lb (1 633 kg)
Max cruising speed (75% power) at 6 500 ft (1 980 m):
170 knots (196 mph; 315 km/h)
Max rate of climb at S/L: 1 015 ft (309 m)/min
Service ceiling: 16 000 ft (4 875 m)
Range (55% power) at 12 000 ft (3 660 m) with optional fuel; with reserves: 769 nm (886 miles; 1 425 km)
Accommodation: Seating for up to six persons. Two rear removable seats and two folding seats permit conversion to utility configuration. As air ambulance, one stretcher plus attendant and/or passenger. Baggage capacity 400 lb (181 kg). Optional dual controls

Variants: (Continental engines in all cases)

A33 Debonair. Initial four-seat version (1961): 225 hp IO-470-J engine. Basically similar airframe to Model 35 Bonanza except for conventional tail unit

B33 Debonair. 1962 version: 225 hp IO-470-K engine

C33 Debonair. 1965 version: enlarged rear cabin windows, redesigned accommodation

C33A Debonair. As C33, with 285 hp IO-520-B engine

F33 (originally E33) Bonanza. 1964 version: 225 hp IO-470-K engine, optional fifth seat. Aerobatic version (1968) designated E33B

F33A (originally E33A) Bonanza. As E33 but with 285 hp IO-520-B engine. Aerobatic version (1968) designated F33C (originally E33C). Production continues of F33A

G33 Bonanza. 1971 version: 260 hp IO-470-N engine, shorter-span wings. In production

A36 Bonanza. 1968 version, as described above: 285 hp IO-520-BA engine, full six-seat capacity. In production

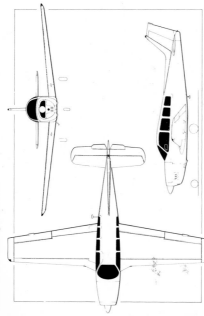

Photo: F33A Bonanza
Drawing: A36 Bonanza
Data: Model A36
Power plant: One IO-520-BA six-cylinder piston engine (285 hp)
Wing span: 33 ft 6 in (10.21 m)
Length overall: 27 ft 6 in (8.38 m)
Cabin: Length: 10 ft 11 in (3.33 m), Height 4 ft 2 in (1.27 m)
Width: 3 ft 6 in (1.07 m)

BEECHCRAFT MODEL 35 BONANZA (V-tail) (USA)

First flight 1945

Four- to six-seat light aircraft

Max T-O weight: 3 400 lb (1 542 kg)

Max cruising speed (75% power) at 6 500 ft (1 980 m): 176 knots (203 mph; 327 km/h)

Max rate of climb at S/L: 1 136 ft (346 m)/min

Service ceiling: 17 500 ft (5 335 m)

Range (75% power) at 6 500 ft (1 980 m) with optional fuel; allowance for warm-up, taxi, take-off and climb with 45 min fuel reserve: 708 nm (816 miles; 1 313 km)

Range (45% power) at 12 000 ft (3 660 m) with optional fuel; reserves as above: 874 nm (1 007 miles, 1 620 km)

Accommodation: Seating for four, five or six persons. Space for up to 270 lb (122.5 kg) of baggage aft of seats

Equipment: Standard equipment includes a 1.7 cu ft (0.05 m³) utility shelf. Optional dual controls

Variants: (Continental engines in all cases)

A35. Initial four-seat version: 185 hp E-185-1 engine
B35. 1950 version
C35. 1951 version: 205 hp E-185-11 engine
D35 and E35. 1953 and 1954 versions
F35. 1955 version: 225 hp E-225-8 engine
G35. 1956 version
H35. 1957 version: 240 hp O-470-G engine
J35. 1958 version: 250 hp IO-470-C engine
K35. 1959 version: optional fifth seat
M35. 1960 version: squared-off wingtips
N35. 1961 version: 260 hp IO-470-H engine
P35. 1962 version: 260 hp IO-470-N engine
S35. 1964 version: 285 hp IO-520-B engine, optional sixth seat, extra cabin windows, redesigned wingtips
V35. 1965 version: redesigned windscreen. In production: current model designated **V35B**

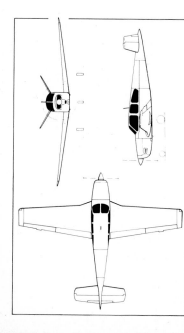

Photo and Drawing: V35B Bonanza

Data: Model V35B

Power plant: One Continental IO-520-BA six-cylinder piston engine (285 hp)

Wing span: 33 ft 6 in (10.21 m)

Length overall: 26 ft 5 in (8.05 m)

Cabin: Length: 8 ft 1 in (2.46 m). Width: 3 ft 6 in (1.07 m). Height: 4 ft 2 in (1.27 m)

Baggage space: 35 cu ft (0.99 m³)

Weight empty, equipped: 2 031 lb (921 kg)

BEECHCRAFT DUKE (USA)

First flight 1966

Light business transport

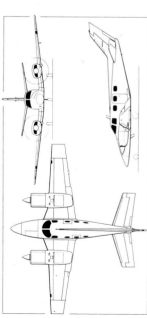

Photo: A60 Duke

Data: Model B60

Power plant: Two Lycoming TIO-541-E1C4 six-cylinder turbocharged piston engines (each 380 hp)

Wing span: 39 ft 3 in (11.96 m)
Length overall: 33 ft 10 in (10.31 m)
Cabin:
Length: 11 ft 10 in (3.61 m)
Width: 4 ft 2 in (1.27 m)
Height: 4 ft 4 in (1.32 m)
Baggage compartment:
front 32 cu ft (0.91 m³)
rear 28.25 cu ft (0.80 m³)
Weight empty, equipped: 4 235 lb (1 921 kg)
Max T-O weight: 6 775 lb (3 073 kg)
Max cruising speed (79% power) at 25 000 ft (7 620 m): 241 knots (278 mph; 447 km/h)
Max rate of climb at S/L: 1 601 ft (488 m)/min
Service ceiling: 30 800 ft (9 390 m)
Range (75% power) at 25 000 ft (7 620 m) with optional fuel; allowances for warm-up, taxi, take-off and climb to altitude with 45 min fuel reserve: 837 nm (963 miles; 1 550 km)
Range (45% power) at 15 000 ft (4 570 m) with optional fuel; allowances as above: 1 023 nm (1 177 miles; 1 893 km)

Accommodation: Standard seating for four persons, in pairs, with optional fifth and sixth seats. Dual controls standard. Baggage hold in nose with a capacity of 500 lb (226 kg), and in rear of cabin with a capacity of 315 lb (143 kg). Optional extras include writing desk, refreshment cabinets and toilet

Variants:
A60. 1971 version: TIO-541-E1A4 engines
B60. 1974 version: as described above. In production

51

First flight 1961 BEECHCRAFT SIERRA/SUNDOWNER/SPORT and MODEL 23 MUSKETEER (USA)

Two- to six-seat light aircraft

Max T-O weight: 2 750 lb (1 247 kg)
Max cruising speed at 7 000 ft (2 135 m), at 2 600 lb (1 179 kg) AUW: 131 knots (151 mph, 243 km/h)
Max rate of climb at S/L: 893 ft (272 m)/min
Service ceiling: 14 350 ft (4 375 m)
Range (75% power) at 7 000 ft (2 135 m) with 52 US gal fuel; allowances for warm-up, etc, with 45 min reserve: 561 nm (646 miles, 1 040 km)
Range (55% power) at 10 000 ft (3 050 m) with 52 US gal fuel; above allowances: 592 nm (682 miles; 1 097 km)
Accommodation: Seating for pilot and three to five passengers. Baggage compartment capacity 270 lb (122 kg)
Equipment: Optional equipment includes factory-installed equipment packages which include dual controls
Variants:

Musketeer I. Initial four-seat version: 160 hp Lycoming O-320-B2C engine.

Musketeer II. Redesigned version (1963): 165 hp Continental IO-346-A engine, extra cabin windows, increased-deflection flaps

Sundowner. Basic four-seat version, first introduced in 1965 as Musketeer III Custom: 165 hp Continental IO-346-A engine. Renamed Sundowner 1971; currently 180 hp Lycoming O-360-A4J engine. In production

Sport. Two-seat (optionally four-seat) sporting and training version, first introduced in 1965 as Musketeer III Sport. Renamed in 1971: 150 hp Lycoming O-320-E2D (originally-E2C) engine. In production

Sierra. Four/six-seat version, first introduced in 1965 as Musketeer III Super. Renamed in 1971: 200 hp Lycoming IO-360-A1B or -A1D (originally-A1A) engine and retractable tricycle landing gear. In production

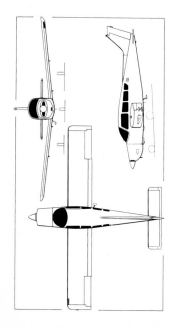

Photo: Sundowner
Drawing: Sierra
Data: Sierra 200 B24R
Power plant: One Lycoming IO-360-A1B four-cylinder piston engine (200 hp)
Wing span: 32 ft 9 in (9.98 m)
Length overall: 25 ft 8½ in (7.84 m)
Cabin, aft of instrument panel:
Length: 7 ft 11 in (2.41 m). Max width: 3 ft 8 in (1.18 m)
Volume: 103.2 cu ft (2.92 m³)
Weight empty (with unusable fuel, oil): 1 771 lb (776 kg)

53

BELL MODEL 47 series (USA)

First flight 1945

Two / three-seat general-purpose helicopter

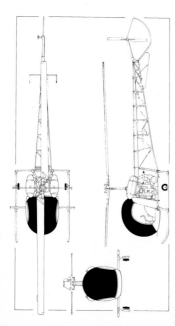

Photo: Model 47G-3B-1
Drawing: Model 47G-2
Data: Model 47G-3B-2A
Power plant: One Lycoming TVO-435-F1A six-cylinder piston engine (280 hp)
Main rotor diameter: 37 ft 1½ in (11.32 m)
Length of fuselage: 31 ft 7 in (9.63 m)
Weight empty, equipped: 1 893 lb (858 kg)
Max T-O weight: 2 950 lb (1 338 kg)
Recommended cruising speed at 5 000 ft (1 525 m): 73 knots (84 mph; 135 km/h)
Max rate of climb at S/L: 990 ft (302 m) / min

Service ceiling: 19 000 ft (5 790 m)
Range with max fuel at 6 000 ft (1 830 m), no reserves: 214 nm (247 miles; 397 km)

Accommodation: Side-by-side seats for three persons. Can carry 1 000 lb (454 kg) of cargo externally

Equipment: AgMaster chemical application system, stretchers, cargo carriers and dual controls optional

Civil variants: Model 47. Pre-production version (10 built): 178 hp Franklin engine, car-type cabin for two
Model 47B. First major civil version: Similar to pre-production version. Available with open cockpit (47B-3)
Model 47D. First version with "goldfish bowl" canopy; openwork tailboom and underfin on three-seat 47D-1
Model 47E. 200 hp Franklin 6V4-200-C32 engine
Model 47G. Combined seating of 47D-1 with engine of 47E. **Models 47G-2 to 47G-5** similar, but various Lycoming engines from 200 to 280 hp, and optional metal rotor blades. 47G series in production since 1953
Model 47H. Generally similar to 47G series, but with fully-enclosed fuselage and car-type cabin: 200 hp Franklin 6V4-200-C32AB engine
Model 47J Ranger (originally 47G-1). Generally similar to 47H, but seating for four persons: 220 hp Lycoming VO-435 engine. Powered controls and metal rotor blades introduced as standard by 47J-2 (260 hp VO-540) in 1960. Agusta versions include 4 / 5-seat 47J-3 (270 hp VO-540) and 47J-3B-1 (270 hp TVO-435). In production
EMA 124. Agusta / Meridionali three-seat development of 47G: 250 hp VO-540. In production
KH-4. Kawasaki four-seat version of 47G-3B. In production

First flights 1956/1961

Utility transport helicopter

BELL MODELS 204/205 (USA)

Length of fuselage: 41 ft 6 in (12.65 m)
Weight empty, equipped: 5 197 lb (2 357 kg)
Normal T-O weight: 9 500 lb (4 309 kg)
Max T-O weight, external load: 10 500 lb (4 763 kg)
Max cruising speed at S/L, at normal T-O weight: 110 knots (127 mph; 204 km/h)
Max rate of climb at S/L, at normal T-O weight: 1 680 ft (512 m)/min
Service ceiling, at normal T-O weight: 14 700 ft (4 480 m)
Range at S/L, at max cruising speed, at normal T-O weight: 270 nm (311 miles; 500 km)
Range at 8 000 ft (2 440 m) at max cruising speed, no reserves, at normal T-O weight: 298 nm (344 miles; 553 km)

Accommodation: Seating for up to 15 persons. Can be rapidly converted to carry freight or be used as a flying crane, ambulance, rescue or executive helicopter. Total cargo capacity 248 cu ft (7.02 m³) including baggage space in tailboom. External load capacity in flying crane role is 5 000 lb (2 268 kg). The ambulance version can accommodate six stretchers and one or two medical attendants. Dual controls optional

Civil variants:
Model 204B. Ten-seat commercial equivalent of UH-1B: 1 100 shp Lycoming T5311A turboshaft as standard in US-built aircraft. Those built by Agusta in Italy available with Rolls-Royce Gnome H.1200 or General-Electric T58-GE-3 as alternative
Model 205A-1. Fifteen-seat commercial equivalent of UH-1H, as described above. In production

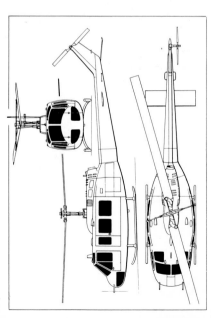

Photo and Drawing: Model 205A-1
Data: Model 205A-1
Power plant: One Lycoming T5313A turboshaft engine (1 400 shp, derated to 1 250 shp for take-off)
Main rotor diameter: 48 ft 0 in (14.63 m)

First flights 1966/1973

Light general-purpose helicopter

BELL MODEL 206 JETRANGER/LONG RANGER (USA)

Length of fuselage: 31 ft 2 in (9.50 m)
Cabin:
  Length: 7 ft 0 in (2.13 m)
  Max width: 4 ft 2 in (1.27 m)
  Max height: 4 ft 3 in (1.28 m)
Baggage compartment volume: 16 cu ft (0.45 m³)
FAA empty weight: 1 455 lb (660 kg)
Max T-O weight: 3 200 lb (1 451 kg)
Max cruising speed at S/L: 118 knots (136 mph; 219 km/h)

Max rate of climb at S/L: 1 260 ft (384 m)/min
Service ceiling: over 20 000 ft (6 100 m)
Range with max fuel and max payload at S/L, no reserves: 299 nm (345 miles; 555 km)
Range with max fuel and max payload at 5 000 ft (1 525 m), no reserves: 337 nm (388 miles; 624 km)
Accommodation: Two seats side by side in front and seating for three persons at rear of cabin. Baggage compartment aft of rear seats, capacity 250 lb (113 kg). Dual controls optional. Optional external cargo sling with 1 200 lb (545 kg) capacity

Civil variants:
Model 206A JetRanger. Initial civil production version: 317 shp Allison 250-C18A turboshaft
Model 206B JetRanger II. More powerful current version described above: superseded 206A in production from 1971
Model 206L Long Ranger. Six/seven-seat version with longer cabin, 420 shp Allison 250-C20B turboshaft, new rotor and Noda-Matic cabin suspension system, and extra fuel. Under development

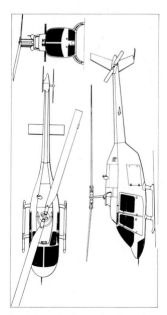

Photo and Drawing: JetRanger
Data: Model 206B JetRanger II
Power plant: One Allison 250-C20 turboshaft engine (400 shp)
Main rotor diameter: 33 ft 4 in (10.16 m)

BELL MODEL 212 TWIN TWO-TWELVE (USA)

First flight 1970

Utility transport helicopter

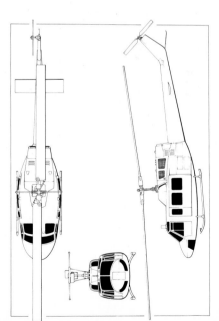

Power plant: One Pratt & Whitney (UACL) PT6T-3 Turbo Twin Pac (two coupled PT6 turboshaft engines, producing 1 800 shp, the Twin Pac flat-rated to 1 250 shp)

Main rotor diameter (with tracking tips): 48 ft 2¼ in (14.69 m)

Length of fuselage: 42 ft 4¾ in (12.92 m)

FAA empty weight plus usable oil: 5 549 lb (2 517 kg)

Max T-O weight: 11 200 lb (5 080 kg)

Max level speed at S/L: 109 knots (126 mph; 203 km/h)

Max rate of climb at S/L: 1 745 ft (532 m)/min

Service ceiling: 17 400 ft (5 305 m)

Max range at S/L, no reserves: 237 nm (273 miles; 439 km)

Accommodation: Pilot and up to 14 passengers or cargo. Internal cargo volume 220 cu ft (6.23 m³). Capable of carrying external load of up to 5 000 lb (2 268 kg)

Civil variants: Standard version, as described above. In production

61

First flight 1971

Two-seat light aircraft

BELLANCA (CHAMPION) 7ACA CHAMP (USA)

Data: Model 7ACA
Power plant: One Franklin 2A-120-B two-cylinder piston engine (60 hp)
Wing span: 35 ft 1½ in (10.71 m)
Length overall: 21 ft 9½ in (6.64 m)
Weight empty: 750 lb (340 kg)
Max T-O weight: 1 220 lb (553 kg)
Max cruising speed (75% power): 72 knots (83 mph; 133 km/h)
Max rate of climb at S/L: 400 ft (122 m)/min
Range with max fuel: 260 nm (300 miles; 483 km)
Accommodation: Seating for two persons in tandem. Dual controls standard. Space for 40 lb (18 kg) of baggage
Variants: Current Model 7ACA, as described above. In production. More than 7 200 built up to 1948 as Aeronca Model 7 AC with 65 hp Continental engine

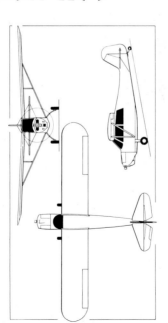

BELLANCA VIKING series (USA)

Wing span: 34 ft 2 in (10.41 m)
Length overall: 23 ft 6 in (7.16 m)
Weight empty: 1 900 lb (862 kg)
Max T-O weight: 3 325 lb (1 508 kg)
Max cruising speed: 163 knots (188 mph; 303 km/h)
Max rate of climb at S/L: 1 840 ft (561 m)/min
Service ceiling: 21 000 ft (6 400 m)
Range with 300 hp Lycoming IO-540 engine and 92 US gallons (348 litres) fuel: 816 nm (940 miles; 1 513 km)
Accommodation: Seating for four persons. Dual controls standard. Space for 186 lb (84 kg) of baggage aft of rear seats

Variants:

Bellanca 260B. Developed from earlier Model 14-19 Cruisemaster, with single sweptback fin and rudder replacing original tail unit

Bellanca 260C. Improved version of 260B: 260 hp Continental IO-470-F

Standard Viking 300. Airframe as 260C, but with 300 hp Continental IO-520-D or 300 hp Lycoming IO-540

Super Viking 300. As Continental-engined Standard 300, but increased fuel and more luxurious appointments. In production

Super Viking 300. As Lycoming-engined Standard 300, but increased fuel and more luxurious appointments. In production

Turbo Viking. As Standard Viking, but 310 hp Lycoming TIO-540 turbocharged engine. Originally known as Standard Turbo Viking 300. In production

65

First flight 1964

Four-seat light business aircraft

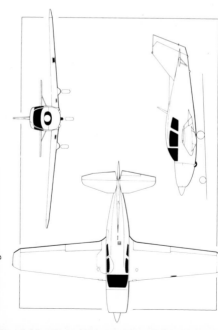

Photo and Drawing: Viking 300
Data: Super Viking 300 (Continental-engined version except where indicated)
Power plant: One Continental IO-520-D six-cylinder piston engine (300 hp)

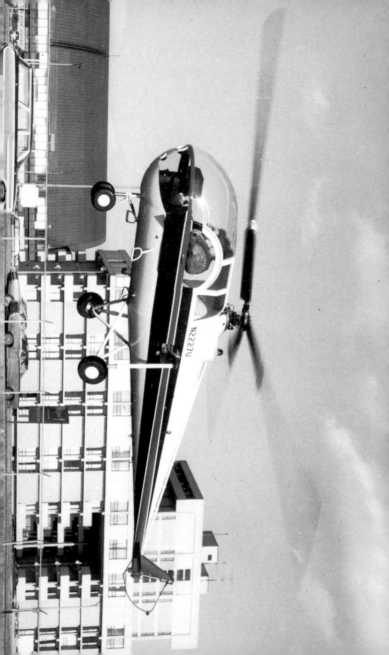

BRANTLY B-2 and 305 (USA)

First flights 1953/1964

Two-seat (B-2) and five-seat (Model 305) light helicopter

Data: B-2B

Power plant: One Lycoming IVO-360-A1A four-cylinder piston engine (180 hp)

Main rotor diameter: 23 ft 9 in (7.24 m)

Length overall: 21 ft 9 in (6.62 m)

Cabin: Max width: 4 ft 2 in (1.27 m)

Weight empty with skids: 1 020 lb (463 kg)

Weight empty with floats: 1 060 lb (481 kg)

Max T-O weight: 1 670 lb (757 kg)

Max cruising speed (75% power): 78 knots (90 mph; 145 km/h)

Max rate of climb at S/L: 1 900 ft (580 m) / min

Service ceiling: 10 800 ft (3 290 m)

Range with max fuel, with reserve: 217 nm (250 miles; 400 km)

Accommodation: Seating for two persons. Dual controls. Baggage compartment, capacity 50 lb (22.7 kg)

Variants:

B-2. Initial production version: 180 hp Lycoming VO-360-A1A engine

B-2A. Improved version: redesigned cabin, more comprehensive equipment

B-2B. Generally similar to B-2A except for fuel-injection engine and increased max T-O weight, as described above

B-2E. Updated version of B-2B: derated 205 hp Lycoming engine, improved door closures and cabin heating system, solid-state instrumentation. Due to resume production in 1974

Model 305. Enlarged (five-seat) development of B-2B: 305 hp Lycoming IVO-540-A1A engine, 28 ft 8 in (8.74 m) main rotor. Due to resume production in 1974

67

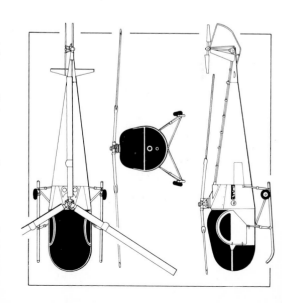

Photo: Model 305
Drawing: B-2

First flight 1934

BÜCKER Bü 131 JUNGMANN (Young Man) (Germany)

Two-seat aerobatic and training biplane

Data: Bü 131B

Power plant: One Hirth HM 504A-2 four-cylinder piston engine (105 hp).

Wing span: 24 ft 3¼ in (7.40 m)

Length overall: 21 ft 8 in (6.60 m)

Weight empty: 837 lb (380 kg)

Max T-O weight: 1 477 lb (670 kg)

Max cruising speed: 92 knots (106 mph; 170 km/h)

Service ceiling: 14 100 ft (4 300 m)

Max range: 350 nm (403 miles; 650 km)

Accommodation: Seating for two persons in tandem, in open cockpits

Variants:

Bü 131A. Initial pre-war production version: 80 hp Hirth HM 60R engine

Bü 131B. Pre-war development of Bü 131A: 105 hp Hirth HM 504A-2 engine

Ki-86. Licence-built wartime version for Japanese Army Air Force with 110 hp Hatsukaze engine; 1 037 built

K9W1. Similar to Ki-86, for Japanese Navy; 217 built

Tatra T-131. Czechoslovakian pre-war licence-built Bü 131B.

Dornier Bü 131B. Swiss pre-war licence-built Bü 131B; 100 built

CASA Bü 131B. Spanish licence-built Bü 131B with 125 hp ENMA Tigre G-IV engine; 200 built

C.4. Czechoslovakian post-war version of Bü 131B

C.104. As C.4 but with 105 hp Walter Minor 4-III engine

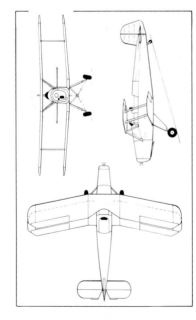

Photo and Drawing: Bü 131B

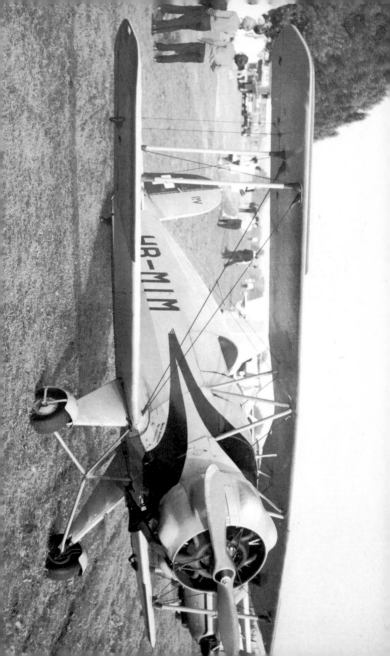

BÜCKER Bü 133 JUNGMEISTER (Young Champion) (Germany)

Single-seat aerobatic and training biplane

Wing span (both wings): 21 ft 7¾ in (6. 60 m)
Length overall: 19 ft 4¼ in (5.90 m)
Weight empty: 925 lb (420 kg)
Max T-O weight: 1 290 lb (585 kg)
Max level speed at 820 ft (250 m): 116 knots (134 mph; 215 km/h)
Max cruising speed at 820 ft (250 m): 108 knots (124 mph; 200 km/h)
Climb to 3 300 ft (1 000 m): 2 min 50 sec
Service ceiling: 19 685 ft (6 000 m)
Range with standard fuel, 6% reserves: 269 nm (310 miles; 500 km)
Accommodation: Single seat in open cockpit. Baggage compartment aft of cockpit
Equipment: Optional equipment includes an 8.6 Imp gallon (39 litre) reserve tank and glider tow hook

Variants:

Bü 133B. Version with 160 hp Hirth HM 506 engine. Limited pre-war production only, in Germany and by CASA in Spain

Bü 133C. Standard version, as described above. Built pre-war in Germany and by Dornier-Altenrhein in Switzerland (47) and CASA in Spain (approx 45)

Bü 133D-1. Re-stressed version of Bü 133C for unlimited aerobatics, built from 1968 by Aero Technik Canary in Germany. Basically as Bü 133C but with power plant installation optimised for constant operation in inverted flight, Goodyear tyres, wheels and brakes, US instrumentation

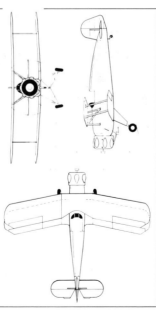

Data: Bü 133C
Power plant: One Siemens Sh 14A-4 seven-cylinder radial piston engine (160 hp)

71

Aerobatic light aircraft

CAARP/MUDRY CAP 10 and 20 (France)

Data: CAP 10
Power plant: One Lycoming IO-360-B2F four-cylinder piston engine (180 hp)
Wing span: 26 ft 5¼ in (8.06 m)
Length overall: 23 ft 11½ in (7.30 m)
Cabin: Max width: 3 ft 5½ in (1.054 m)
Weight empty, equipped: 1 168 lb (530 kg)
Max T-O weight:
  Aerobatic: 1 666 lb (756 kg)
  Utility: 1 829 lb (830 kg)
Max cruising speed (75% power): 129 knots (149 mph; 240 km/h)
Max rate of climb at S/L: over 1 180 ft (360 m)/min
Service ceiling: over 18 050 ft (5 500 m)
Range: 647 nm (745 miles; 1 200 km)
Accommodation: Two seats side by side. Space for 44 lb (20 kg) of baggage aft of seats in training and touring models
Variants:
  CAP 10. Standard two-seat version, as described above. In production
  CAP 20. Single-seat derivative of CAP 10
  CAP 20A. Single-seat derivative of CAP 10, with no-dihedral wings and lightened landing gear. In production
  CAP 20B. Modified CAP 20A with new wings and larger ailerons: under development
  CAP 20C, D and E. Further-modified versions, under development

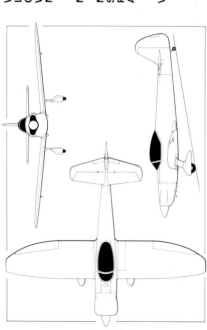

Photo and Drawing: CAP 20

73

First flight 1967

Single / four-seat light aircraft

CASA / MBB 223 FLAMINGO (Spain / Germany)

Weight empty, equipped: 1 510 lb (685 kg)
Max T-O weight (Normal category): 2 315 lb (1 050 kg)
Max cruising speed (75% power), category as above: 116 knots (134 mph; 216 km/h)
Max rate of climb at S/L, category as above: 846 ft (258 m)/min
Service ceiling, category as above: 12 300 ft (3 750 m)
Range with 30 min reserves, category as above: 475 nm (547 miles; 880 km)
Range with max fuel, category as above: 620 nm (715 miles; 1 150 km)
Accommodation: Two seats side by side at front of cabin with provision for fitting a folding seat for one adult or two children in the baggage area. Space for 200 lb (90 kg) of baggage aft of front seats when used as a two-seat utility aircraft. Removable dual controls. Can also be equipped (Normal category) as an agricultural aircraft, for dispensing liquid or dry chemicals

Variants:

CASA (originally SIAT) 223A1. Basic version, available in Normal category as three / four-seat touring aircraft (as described above) or agricultural aircraft, or in Utility category as a two-seater intended primarily for training airline pilots. In production (originally in Germany), currently in Spain)

CASA (originally SIAT) 223K1. Single-seat fully-aerobatic version with specially-modified IO-360-C1B engine and stressed to +6g and −4g. In production (originally in Germany, currently in Spain)

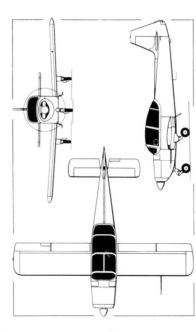

Data: CASA 223A1
Power plant: One Lycoming IO-360-C1B four-cylinder piston engine (200 hp)
Wing span: 27 ft 2 in (8.28 m)
Length overall: 24 ft 4½ in (7.43 m)
Cabin:
Length: 7 ft 2½ in (2.20 m)
Width: 3 ft 8 in (1.12 m)
Height: 3 ft 11¼ in (1.20 m)

75

CERVA CE.43 GUÉPARD (CHEETAH) (France)

Power plant: One Lycoming IO-540-C4B5 six-cylinder piston engine (250 hp)
Wing span: 32 ft 9½ in (10.00 m)
Length overall: 27 ft 6½ in (8.40 m)
Cabin: Max width: 3 ft 7 in (1.09 m)
Weight empty: 1 863 lb (845 kg)
Max T-O weight:
 Utility: 3 220 lb (1 460 kg)
 Normal: 3 527 lb (1 600 kg)
Max cruising speed: 167 knots (192 mph; 310 km/h)
Max rate of climb at S/L: 1 080 ft (330 m)/min
Service ceiling: 17 400 ft (5 300 m)
Range with max fuel: 1 565 nm (1 800 miles; 2 900 km)
Accommodation: Two seats side by side at front, with dual controls. Rear bench seat for two persons. Baggage compartment aft of cabin
Variants: Standard version, as described above. In production. Six-seat version with Tiara engine flown 1974; light cargo-carrying version, projected

First flight 1971

Four-seat light aircraft

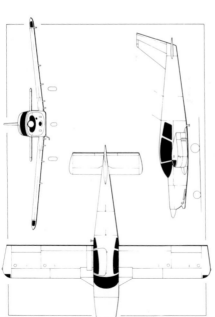

CESSNA 150 (USA)

First flight 1957

Two-seat light aircraft

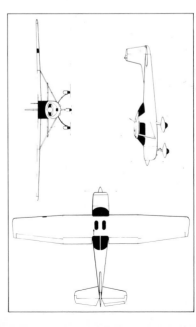

Photo: F.150
Drawing: Model 150 D
Data: 1974 Model 150
Power plant: One Continental 0-200-A four-cylinder piston engine (100 hp)
Wing span: Standard, trainer 32ft 8½ in (9.97 m), commuter 33ft 2 in (10.11 m)
Length overall: Standard 23 ft 0 in (7.01 m), trainer, commuter 23ft 9 in (7.24 m).

Weight empty, equipped, standard tanks: Standard 990 lb (449 kg), trainer 1,010 lb (458 kg), commuter 1,060 lb (480 kg)
Max T-O weight: 1,600 lb (726 kg)
Max cruising speed (75% power) at 7,000 ft (2,133 m): 102 knots (117 mph; 188 km/h)
Max rate of climb at S/L: 670 ft (204 m) / min
Service ceiling: 12 650 ft (3 850 m)
Range at speed of 81 knots (93 mph;149 km/h), normal fuel, no reserve: 490 nm (565 miles; fuel 909 km)
Range at max cruising speed, long-range tanks, no reserve: 629 nm (725 miles; 1 166 km)
Accommodation: Seating for two persons side by side. Dual controls standard in trainer and commuter, optional in standard model. Baggage compartment behind seats, capacity 120 lb (54 kg), or ''family seat'' in space

Variants:
Model 150A, B and C. Initial versions (1958-63), differing in detail only. Non-swept fin and rudder. Rear ''family seat'' introduced on 150C
Model 150D. 1964: wrap-round rear cabin window, slight increase in gross weight. **Model 150E** similar
Model 150F. 1966: first with sweptback fin and rudder
Model 150G. 1967: shorter nosewheel leg, wider cabin
Model 150H. 1968: revised flaps, refined interior
Model 150J. 1969: interior refinements
Model 150K. 1970: conical-camber glassfibre wingtips, ground-adjustable rudder trim tab. Aerobatic version, **A150K Aerobat:** Introduced in 1970. In production
F-150 and FA-150 Aerobat. Designation of aircraft assembled or built in France by Reims Aviation

CESSNA 172/182 and REIMS ROCKET (USA/France)

First Flights 1955/1956/1963

Four-seat light aircraft

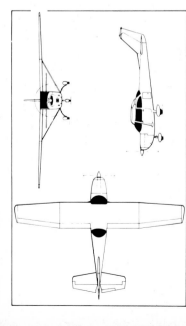

Photo: Skylane
Drawing: Model 172
Data: Model 182
Power plant: One Continental O-470-R six-cylinder piston engine (230 hp)
Wing span: 35 ft 10 in (10.92 m)
Length overall: 28 ft 2 in (8.59 m)
Weight empty, equipped: 1 595 lb (723 kg)
Max T-O weight: 2 950 lb (1 338 kg)

Max cruising speed (75% power) at 6 500 ft (1 980 m): 136 knots (157 mph; 253 km/h)

Max rate of climb at S/L: 890 ft (271 m)/min

Service ceiling: 17 700 ft (5 395 m)

Range at econ cruising speed of 97 knots (112 mph; 180 km/h), with long-range fuel tanks, no reserve: 1 007 nm (1 160 miles; 1 865 km)

Accommodation: Seating for four persons, in pairs. Baggage space aft of rear seats, capacity 200 lb (91 kg)

Equipment: Optional equipment includes dual controls, control wheel, stretcher installation, utility shelf, glider tow hook and a detachable glassfibre cargo pack that is 9 ft long and 2 ft 7 in wide (2.75 m × 0.79 m)

Variants:
Model 172 (initial version, derived from Model 170), Model 172A (1960), Model 172B (later 1960), Model 172C (1962) Model 172D (1963) Models 172 F and G (1964 and 1966), Model 172H (1967), Model 172I (1968), Model 172K (1969; remains in production 1974; De Luxe version known as Skyhawk available from 172B onwards), Rocket (versions built in France by Reims Aviation; F-172, FR-172 current version, FRA-172 STOL version), F-172, Model 182, Model 182A, Model 182B, Model 182C (1960), Model 182D (1961), Model 182E (1962), Model 182F (1963), Model 182G (1964), Model 182H (1965), Model 182J (1966) Model 182K (1967), Model 182L (1968), Model 182M (1969; remains in production 1974; De Luxe version known as Skylane available from 1958 onwards)

CESSNA 177/CARDINAL/CARDINAL RG (USA)

First flights 1967/1970

Four-seat light aircraft

Weight empty, equipped: 1 450 lb (657 kg)
Max T-O weight: 2 500 lb (1 133 kg)
Max cruising speed (75% power) at 8 000 ft (2 440 m), with wheel fairings: 124 knots (143 mph: 230 km/h)
Max rate of climb at S/L: 840 ft (256 m)/min
Service ceiling: 14 600 ft (4 450 m)
Range at max cruising speed, standard fuel, no reserve: 603 nm (695 miles: 1 118 km)
Range at econ cruising speed of 109 knots (125 mph: 201 km/h), optional fuel, no reserve: 838 nm (965 miles: 1 553 km)
Accommodation: Seating for four persons. Optional seat for two children aft of rear seats. Baggage compartment in rear fuselage, capacity 120 lb (54 kg)
Equipment: Optional equipment includes dual controls, children's seat and stretcher

Variants:

Model 177. Standard initial version from 1967: 150 hp Lycoming O-320-E21D engine. Continues in production 1974, incorporating such refinements as 180 hp Lycoming O-360 and upswept tailcone (1969 Model 177A), gull-wing leading-edge and conical-camber wingtips (1970 Model 177B), and optional extra fuel (1973)

Cardinal. De luxe version of 177 from 1967. Continues in production 1974, incorporating same refinements as standard 177

Cardinal RG. Retractable landing gear version with 200 hp Lycoming AIO-360-A1A engine, introduced Dec. 1970. Continues in production 1974, incorporating new propeller and engineering refinements (1972) and optional extra fuel (1973)

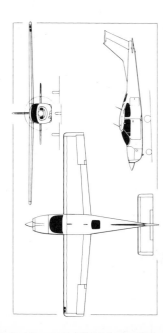

Photo and Drawing: Cardinal RG
Data: Model 177
Power plant: One Lycoming O-360-A1F6 four-cylinder piston engine (180 hp)
Wing span: 35 ft 6 in (10.82 m)
Length overall: 27 ft 3 in (8.31 m)
Cabin:
  Length: 14 ft 7½ in (4.46 m)
  Max width: 4 ft 0 in (1.22 m)
  Max height: 3 ft 8½ in (1.13 m)

First flight 1965 CESSNA MODEL 188 AGPICKUP, AGWAGON and AGTRUCK (USA)

Single-seat agricultural aircraft

Weight empty, with liquid dispersal system, gate box and engine-driven hydraulic pump: 2 040 lb (925 kg)
Gross T-O weight, Normal category: 3 300 lb (1 496 kg)
Max T-O weight, Restricted category: 4 000 lb (1 814 kg)
Max cruising speed (75% power) at 3 300 lb (1 496 kg) AUW, at 6 500 ft (1 980 m): 122 knots (141 mph; 227 km/h)
Max rate of climb at S/L, AUW as above: 940 ft (287 m)/min
Service ceiling, AUW as above: 15 700 ft (4 785 m)
Range (75% power), standard fuel, no reserve, AUW as above, at 6 500 ft (1 980 m): 278 nm (320 miles; 515 km)
Range (75% power), long-range fuel, no reserve, AUW as above: 338 nm (390 miles; 625 km)

Accommodation: Single seat in enclosed cockpit
Equipment: Standard equipment includes a 200 US gallon (757 litre) hopper, and liquid and dry material dispersal control system. Optional equipment includes 22, 44 or 64 nozzle spraybooms and two spreader systems for either medium or high-volume applications

Variants:
AGpickup (originally Agwagon 230). Basic version: 230 hp Continental O-470-R engine. In production
AGwagon (originally Agwagon 300). As AGpickup but 300 hp Continental IO-520-D engine, as described above. In production
AGtruck. As AGwagon but 280 US gallon (1 060 litre) hopper, standard 22-nozzle spray system, wing fuel tanks, conical-camber wingtips, oversize tyres and other additional standard features. In production

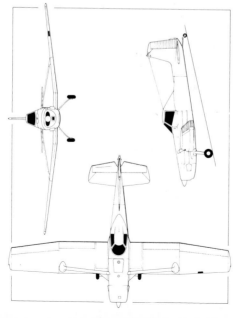

Photo and Drawing: AGwagon

Data: AGwagon
Power plant: One Continental IO-520-D six-cylinder piston engine (300 hp)
Wing span: 40 ft 8½ in (12.41 m)

CESSNA STATIONAIR (USA)

First flight 1963 (Super Skywagon)

Six-seat cargo/utility light aircraft

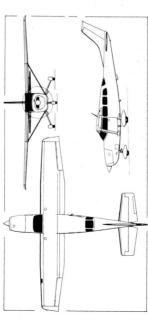

Photo: Stationair
Drawing: Cessna Model 207

Data: Stationair (landplane)
Power plant: One Continental IO-520-F six-cylinder piston engine (300 hp)
Wing span: 35 ft 10 in (10.92 m)

Length overall: 28 ft 0 in (8.53 m)
Cabin:
  Length: 12 ft 0 in (3.66 m)
  Max width: 3 ft 8 in (1.12 m)
  Max height: 4 ft 1½ in (1.26 m)
  Volume available for payload: 101.2 cu ft (2.87 m³)
Weight empty, one seat only: 1 730 lb (784 kg)
Max T-O weight: 3 600 lb (1 633 kg)
Max cruising speed (75% power) at 6 500 ft (1 980 m): 142 knots (164 mph; 264 km/h)
Max rate of climb at S/L: 920 ft (280 m)/min
Service ceiling: 14 800 ft (4 510 m)
Range (75% power), normal fuel, no reserve, at 6 500 ft (1 980 m): 564 nm (650 miles; 1 045 km)
Range at econ cruising speed of 114 knots (131 mph; 211 km/h), long-range tanks, no reserve, at 10 000 ft (3 050 m): 885 nm (1 020 miles; 1 640 km)
Accommodation: Seating for pilot, co-pilot and up to four passengers. Aircraft can be used for cargo carrying or be flown with cargo doors removed for photography, air dropping of supplies or parachuting
Equipment: Optional equipment includes utility shelf, glider tow hook, ambulance kit, casket kit, photographic provisions and skydiving kit
Variants:
Stationair (originally U206 Super Skywagon). Standard cargo utility model, as described above. In production. Stretched version known as Cessna 207
Turbo-Stationair (originally TU 206 Turbo-Skywagon). Similar to Stationair but 285 hp Continental TSIO-520-C engine, modified cowling. In production

First flight 1957

Six-seat light aircraft

CESSNA 210 CENTURION (USA)

Max cruising speed (75% power) at 7 500 ft (2 285 m): 163 knots (188 mph; 303 km/h)

Max rate of climb at S/L: 860 ft (262 m)/min

Service ceiling: 15 500 ft (4 725 m)

Range at max cruising speed, standard fuel, no reserves: 925 nm (1 065 miles; 1 713 km)

Accommodation: Seating for six persons, in pairs. Fifth and sixth seats have folding backs to permit carriage of articles up to 6 ft 7 in long. Optional four-seat interior. Dual controls standard. Baggage capacity 300 lb (136 kg).

Variants: Model 210. Initial four-seat version (1960): 260 hp Continental IO-470-S engine, strut-braced wings

Model 210A. 1961: larger cabin windows, plus two extra

Model 210B. 1962: fuselage cut down at rear

Model 210C. 1963: improved cabin appointments

Model 210D. 1964: 285 hp Continental IO-520-A engine

Model 210E. 1965: modified engine cowling; 1966

Model 210F similar

Model 210G. 1967: fully-cantilevered wings; 1968

Model 210H similar, with improved instrumentation. Suffix letter system then dropped. 1969 version introduced longer, restyled nose cowling, larger dorsal fin, reduced engine dihedral. Seating increased to six in 1970

Model 210 Centurion I and II. 1971 designations for std models, differing in avionics and some cabin appointments. Engine change to 10-520-L, 1972. In production 1974.

T210 Turbo-Centurion I and II (originally Turbo-System Centurion). These turbocharged versions have paralleled standard Centurion production from 1960, and currently have 285 hp Continental TSIO-520-H engine

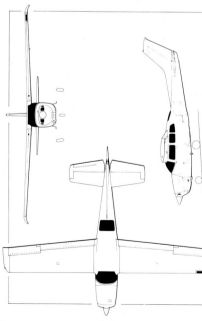

Photo and Drawing: T210 Turbo-Centurion II

Data: Model 210 Centurion II

Power plant: One Continental IO-520-L six-cylinder piston engine (300 hp)

Wing span: 36 ft 9 in (11.20 m)

Length overall: 28 ft 3 in (8.61 m)

Weight empty: approx 2 205 lb (1 000 kg)

Max T-O weight: 3 800 lb (1 723 kg)

CESSNA 310/340 (USA)

First flights 1953/1972

Six-seat light business transport

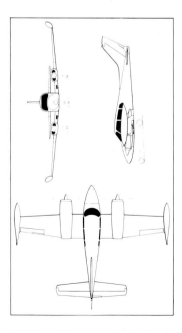

Photo: Model 310 (1974)
Drawing: Model 310J

Data: Model 340
Power plant: Two Continental TSIO-520-K six-cylinder turbocharged piston engines (each 285 hp)

Wing span: 38 ft 1.3 in (11.62 m)
Length overall: 34 ft 4 in (10.46 m)
Cabin: Length, incl baggage compartment: 12 ft 8 in (3.86 m). Max width: 3 ft 10½ in (1.18 m). Max height: 4 ft 1 in (1.24 m). Volume: 162.4 cu ft (4.6 m³)
Weight empty: approx 3 723 lb (1 688 kg)
Max T-O weight: 5 975 lb (2 710 kg)
Max cruising speed (75% power) at 20 000 ft (6 100 m): 209 knots (241 mph; 388 km/h)
Max rate of climb at S/L: 1 500 ft (457 m)/min
Service ceiling: 26 500 ft (8 075 m)
Range (75% power) at 10 000 ft (3 050 m), with 600 lb (272 kg) fuel, no reserve: 575 nm (663 miles; 1 067 km)
Max range at econ cruising speed of 175 knots (202 mph; 325 km/h), with 1 218 lb (552 kg) fuel, no reserve: 1 402 nm (1 615 miles; 2 600 km)
Accommodation: Seating for pilot, co-pilot and four passengers. Baggage compartment in nose, capacity 350 lb (159 kg): two wing lockers, capacity 120 lb (54.5 kg) each; and in rear cabin area, capacity 340 lb (154 kg)
Civil variants:
Model 310 (initial 1954 version), Model 310B (1957), Model 310C (1959), Model 310D (1960), Model 310F (1961), Model 310G (1962), Model 310H (1963), Model 310I (1964), Model 310J (1965), Model 310K (1966), Model 310L (1967), Model 310N (1968), Model 310P (1969), Model 310Q (1970: production continues), Turbo-System T310 (introduced 1969 as Turbo-System 310P. Replaced Model 320 Skyknight of which 509 built 1961-68. In production). Model 340 (introduced 1972, in production)

CESSNA 337 SKYMASTER (USA)

First flight 1965

Four- to six-seat light transport

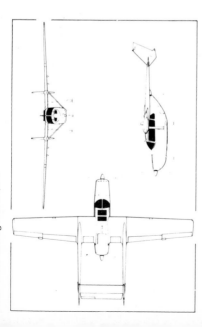

Photo and Drawing: Model 337 Skymaster

Data: Standard commercial Model 337
Power plant: Two Continental IO-360-C six-cylinder piston engines (each 210 hp)
Wing span: 38 ft 2 in (11.63 m)

Length overall: 29 ft 9 in (9.07 m)
Cabin: Length: 9 ft 11 in (3.02 m), Max width: 3 ft 8¼ in (1.12 m), Max height: 4 ft 3¼ in (1.30 m), Volume: 138 cu ft (3.91 m³)
Range at max cruising speed, standard fuel, no reserve: 677 nm (780 miles: 1 255 km)
Accommodation: Standard seating for pilot, co-pilot and two passengers, in pairs. Alternative arrangements provide for three or four passengers. Space for 365 lb (165 kg) of baggage in four-seat version. Provision for under-fuselage cargo pack, capacity of 300 lb (136 kg)
Equipment: Optional equipment includes dual controls, stretcher, and photographic provisions
Civil variants:

Model 337 Skymaster (originally Super Skymaster). Development of earlier fixed-gear Model 336 Skymaster (195 built), introduced 1965. Successive refinements include increased gross weight (1968 Model 337C), improved instrumentation (1969 Model 337D), further-increased gross weight and conical-camber glassfibre wingtips (1970), seat belts and other safety features (1971), improved cabin layout (1972), detail airframe improvements (1973). In production

Turbo-System Super Skymaster. As standard model but 210 hp Continental TSIO-360-A/B turbocharged engines. Introduced 1967; refinements as for standard model until 1972, after which discontinued

Model T337 Pressurised Skymaster. Similar to standard model but 225 hp Continental TSIO-360 turbocharged engines and pressurised cabin. Introduced 1972: in production

93

CESSNA 401/402 (USA)

First flights 1965/1966

Light business and general-purpose transport

Max T-O weight: 6 300 lb (2 857 kg)
Max cruising speed (75% power) at 10 000 ft (3 050 m): 189 knots (218 mph; 351 km/h)
Max rate of climb at S/L: 1 610 ft (491 m)/min
Service ceiling: 26 180 ft (7 980 m)
Max range at 25 000 ft (7 620 m), with 1 218 lb (552 kg) fuel, no reserve: 1 423 nm (1 639 miles; 2 637 km)

Accommodation: Two seats side by side in pilot's compartment. Seating in Utililiner for eight passengers in main cabin. Businessliner has four seats as standard, with two additional seats optional, in main cabin. Baggage area, at rear of cabin, capacity 500 lb (227 kg). Nose baggage compartment, capacity 350 lb (159 kg). Avionics or baggage compartment in nose, separate from baggage compartment, capacity 250 lb (113 kg). Wing lockers, at rear of each engine nacelle, capacity 120 lb (54 kg) each.

Equipment: Optional equipment includes dual controls and various seats, tables, refreshment units and toilets

Variants:
Models 401 and 402. Introduced late 1966: fundamentally similar airframe and power plant. Model 401 cabin in six/eight-seat executive layout. Model 402 as nine-seat commuter convertible to cargo transport, though both with optional cargo door. Subsequent changes include extended nose on 1969 **Model 402A**, improved cabin seats on 1970 **Model 401B**, seat belts and other safety features (1971, both). Production of Model 401 ended 1972, from which year Model 402 became available as **Utililiner** (basic nine/ten-seater) or **Businessliner** (optional six- or eight-seater). Both of these remain in production, with longer cabin from 1973

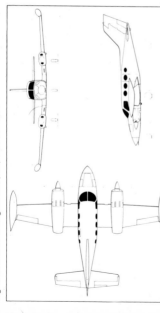

Photo: Model 402 Businessliner
Drawing: Model 401B
Data: Model 402
Power plant: Two Continental TSIO-520-E six-cylinder turbocharged piston engines (each 300 hp)
Wing span over tip-tanks: 39 ft 10¼ in (12.15 m)
Length overall: 36 ft 1 in (11.00 m)
Cabin: Length: 15 ft 10 in (4.83 m), Max width: 4 ft 8 in (1.42 m), Max height: 4 ft 3 in (1.30 m), Volume: 222.4 cu ft (6.30 m³)
Weight empty:
Utililiner: 3 738 lb (1 695 kg)
Businessliner: 3 728 lb (1 691 kg)

CHAMPION (BELLANCA) CITABRIA (USA)

First flight 1964

Two-seat light aircraft

Data: Model 7GCAA
Power plant: One Lycoming O-320-A2B four-cylinder piston engine (150 hp)
Wing span: 33 ft 5 in (10.19 m)
Length overall: 22 ft 8 in (6.91 m)
Weight empty, equipped: 1 037 lb (470 kg)
Max T-O weight: 1 650 lb (748 kg)
Max cruising speed (75% power), at 8 000 ft (2 440 m): 109 knots (125 mph; 201 km/h)
Max rate of climb at S/L: 1 120 ft (341 m)/min
Service ceiling: 17 000 ft (5 180 m)
Range at max cruising speed (39 US gallons fuel): 465 nm (537 miles; 865 km)
Accommodation: Seating for two persons in tandem. Dual controls. Space for 100 lb (45 kg) of baggage

Variants:

Model 7ECA. Basic version, with 115 hp Lycoming O-235-C1 engine and standard wings. Available also as floatplane. In production

Model 7GCAA. As described above: generally similar to Model 7ECA except for power plant. In production

Model 7GCBC Scout. Utility version, generally similar to Model 7ECA but with O-320-A2B engine and wing flaps. Crop-spraying gear available optionally. In production

Model 7KCAB. Generally similar to Model 7ECA but with 150 hp Lycoming IO-320-E2A engine and provision for prolonged inverted flying. In production

Model 8KCAB Decathlon. Developed version of Citabria, cleared for unlimited aerobatics: 150 hp Lycoming IO-320-E1A. In production

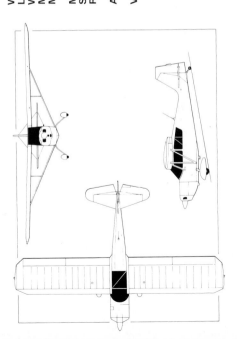

Photo: Model 7GCBC Scout
Drawing: Citabria

DASSAULT FALCON 10 (France)

First flight 1970

Executive light transport

Data: Prototype

Power plant: Two Garrett AiResearch TFE 731-2 turbofan engines (each 3 230 lb; 1 465 kg st)

Wing span: 42 ft 11 in (13.08 m)

Length overall: 45 ft 5 in (13.85 m)

Cabin, excluding flight deck:
Length: 16 ft 5 in (5.00 m)
Max width: 4 ft 9 in (1.46 m)
Max height: 4 ft 11 in (1.50 m)
Volume: 264.6 cu ft (7.50 m³)

Baggage compartment volume:
front (wardrobe): 12.35 cu ft (0.35 m³)
rear: 24.7 cu ft (0.70 m³)

Weight empty, equipped: 10 416 lb (4 725 kg)

Max payload: 1 945 lb (886 kg)

Max T-O weight: 18 300 lb (8 300 kg)

Max operating Mach number: 0.87

Range with four passengers and 45 min reserves: 1 800 nm (2 070 miles; 3 330 km)

Accommodation: Flight crew of two or three and seating for up to seven passengers. Baggage compartment behind cabin. Can also be used for ambulance, training, navaid calibration and aerial photography duties

Variants: Standard version, equipped according to role; production aircraft will be available eventually with Turbomeca Larzac turbofans

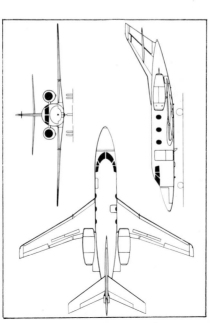

EMBRAER EMB-200 IPANEMA (Brazil)

First flight 1970

Single-seat agricultural aircraft

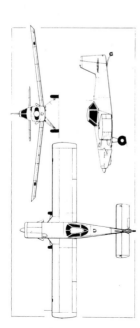

Photo: EMB-200
Drawing: EMB-201

Data: EMB-200
Power plant: One Lycoming O-540-H2B5D six-cylinder piston engine (260 hp)
Wing span: 36 ft 9 in (11.20 m)

Length overall: 24 ft 4½ in (7.43 m)
Cockpit:
Max length: 3 ft 11¼ in (1.20 m)
Max width: 2 ft 9½ in (0.85 m)
Max height: 4 ft 4¾ in (1.34 m)
Max payload:
Normal: 1 212 lb (550 kg)
Restricted: 1 763 lb (800 kg)
Max T-O weight:
Normal: 3 417 lb (1 550 kg)
Restricted: 3 968 lb (1 800 kg)
Cruising speed (67% power), at max Normal T-O weight: 114 knots (131 mph; 211 km/h)
Max rate of climb at S/L, at max Normal T-O weight: 705 ft (215 m)/min
Range with max fuel, no reserves, at max Normal T-O weight: 507 nm (584 miles; 941 km)
Accommodation: Single seat
Equipment: Hopper for agricultural chemicals has capacity of 149.5 Imp gallons (680 litres). Transland dusting system below centre of fuselage. Transland or Micronair spraybooms aft of and above wing trailing-edges
Variants:
EMB-200. Initial production version, as described above
EMB-200A. As EMB-200 but with constant-speed instead of fixed-pitch propeller
EMB-201. Current (1974) version with 300 hp Lycoming IO-540-K1D5 engine and constant-speed propeller. In production
EMB-210 Formigão. Extensively redesigned and enlarged version, with 400 hp Lycoming IO-720-A1A engine and three-blade constant-speed propeller: prototype only

101

ENSTROM F-28 (USA)

First flight 1962

Three-seat light helicopter

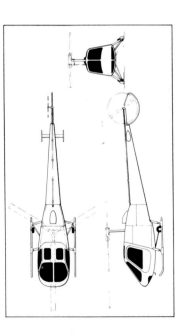

Data: F-28A

Power plant: One Lycoming HIO-360-C1A four-cylinder piston engine (205 hp)

Main rotor diameter: 32 ft 0 in (9.75 m)

Length overall: 29 ft 6 in (8.99 m)

Cabin:

Max width: 5 ft 1 in (1.55 m)

Baggage hold volume: 8 cu ft (0.23 m³)

Weight empty: 1 450 lb (657 kg)

Max T-O weight: 2 150 lb (975 kg)

Max cruising speed at S/L: 87 knots (100 mph; 161 km/h)

Max rate of climb at S/L: 950 ft (290 m)/min

Service ceiling: 12 000 ft (3 660 m)

Range with max fuel: 205 nm (237 miles; 381 km)

Accommodation: Pilot and two passengers, side by side on bench seat. Baggage space aft of engine compartment

Equipment: Optional equipment includes a cargo hook or stretchers

Variants:

F-28. Initial production version

F-28A. Major version, as described above. In production

F-28B. Experimental version: 225 hp Lycoming TIO-360 turbocharged engine

T-28. Experimental version: 240 shp AiResearch TSE 36-1 turboshaft engine, increased fuel, larger-diameter tail rotor, new transmission system

Model 280 Shark. Similar to F-28A but with 205 hp Lycoming turbocharged engine, fuel capacity increased from 30 to 40 US gallons (113 to 151 litres), fixed vertical tail-fin with sweptback upper and ventral sections. Under development

Photo and Drawing: F-28A

ERCOUPE / AIRCOUPE / CADET series (USA)

First flight 1937

Two-seat light aircraft

Max cruising speed (75% power): 105 knots (121 mph; 195 km/h)

Service ceiling: 15 500 ft (4 725 m)

Range: 434 nm (500 miles; 805 km)

Accommodation: Seating for two persons side by side, with space behind for an extra seat suitable for a child weighing up to 75 lb (34 kg) or for 75 lb of baggage

Variants:

Model 415C Ercoupe. Initial Erco-built production version, built 1940-41 with 65 hp Continental A65 engine and 1945-47 with 75 hp Continental C75-12F

Model 415E Ercoupe. Post-war (1947) Erco version: 85 hp Continental C85-12 engine

Model 415F Ercoupe. Post-war (1947) Erco version: 85 hp Continental C85-12J engine

Model 415G Club-Air. Post-war (1949-51) Erco version: 85 hp Continental C85-12 engine

F-1 AirCoupe. Forney-built version (1955-59): 95 hp Continental C90-12F engine. Also known, according to equipment fitted, as **Execta**, **Expediter** and **Explorer**

F-1A AirCoupe. Air Products version (1960-62)

Air-Coupe 415D Club Trainer. Modified F-1A, marketed by Air Products

A-2 AirCoupe. Alon-built version (1964-67): 90 hp Continental C90-16F engine, fully-transparent sliding "bubble" canopy, lower cabin sides

A-2A Cadet. Mooney-built version of A-2 (1967-68): cantilever spring steel main-wheel legs

M-10 Cadet. Final version (1968-69), evolved by Mooney: new rear fuselage and single fin and rudder

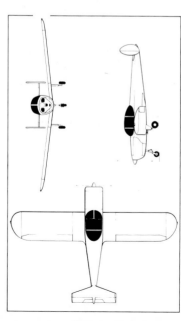

Photo: F-1 AirCoupe
Drawing: A-2 AirCoupe
Data: Forney F-1 AirCoupe
Power plant: One Continental C90-12F four-cylinder piston engine (90 hp)
Wing span: 30 ft 0 in (9.14 m)
Length overall: 20 ft 2 in (6.15 m)
Weight empty: 890 lb (404 kg)
Max T-O weight: 1 400 lb (635 kg)

FFA AS.202 BRAVO (Switzerland)

First flight 1969

Two/three-seat light aircraft

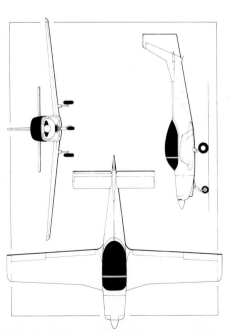

Data: AS.202/15
Power plant: One Lycoming O-320-E2A four-cylinder piston engine (150 hp)
Wing span: 31 ft 11¾ in (9.75 m)
Length overall: 24 ft 7¼ in (7.50 m)
Cabin:
Max length: 7 ft 0½ in (2.15 m)
Max width: 3 ft 4¼ in (1.02 m)
Max height: 3 ft 7¼ in (1.10 m)
Weight empty, equipped: 1 388 lb (630 kg)
Max payload (Utility version): 595 lb (270 kg)
Max T-O weight (Utility version): 2 202 lb (999 kg)
Max cruising speed (75% power) at 8 000 ft (2 440 m) (Utility version): 114 knots (131 mph; 211 km/h)
Max rate of climb at S/L (Utility version): 633 ft (193 m)/min
Service ceiling (Utility version): 14 000 ft (4 265 m)
Range with max fuel, no reserves (Utility version): 498 nm (574 miles; 925 km)
Accommodation: Two seats side by side. Space at rear in Utility version for a third seat or 220 lb (100 kg) of baggage. Dual controls standard
Variants:
AS.202/15. Two/three-seat initial production version, as described above. In production

FMA (DINFIA) IA 46 RANQUEL (Argentine Republic)

First flight 1957

Three-seat light aircraft

Data: Model 66 Ranquel
Power plant: One Lycoming O-320-A2B four-cylinder piston engine (150 hp)
Wing span: 38 ft 1½ in (11.62 m)
Length overall: 24 ft 5 in (7.45 m)
Weight empty, equipped:
Tourer: 1 390 lb (630 kg)
Agricultural: 1 520 lb (690 kg)
Max T-O weight:
Tourer: 2 115 lb (960 kg)
Agricultural: 2 555 lb (1 160 kg)
Max cruising speed (75% power) (Tourer): 83 knots (96 mph; 155 km/h)
Max rate of climb at S/L (Tourer): 470 ft (144 m)/min
Service ceiling (Tourer): 13 125 ft (4 000 m)
Range with max fuel (75% power) (Tourer): 351 nm (405 miles; 650 km)
Accommodation: Seating for pilot in front and two passengers on bench seat aft. Tandem dual controls optional. Baggage compartment behind rear seat
Equipment: A quickly-installed and jettisonable 88 Imp gallon (400 litre) belly tank for agricultural chemicals can be attached without encroaching on passenger space inside cabin
Variants:
Ranquel. Standard production version, as described above
Super Ranquel. Similar to Ranquel but 180 hp Lycoming O-360-A2A engine

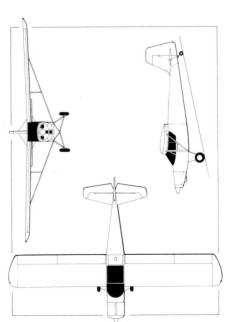

Photo and Drawing: Ranquel

109

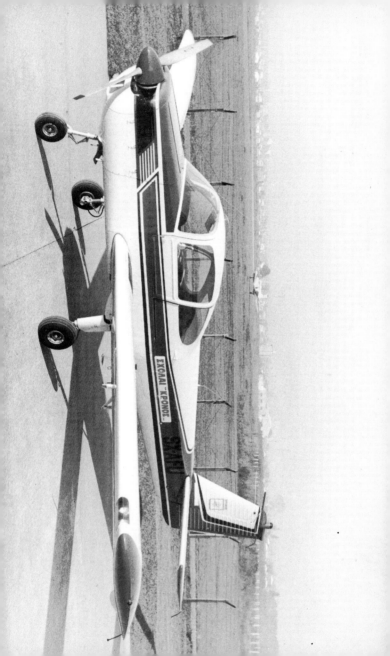

FUJI FA-200 AERO SUBARU (Japan)

First flight 1965

Two / four-seat light aircraft

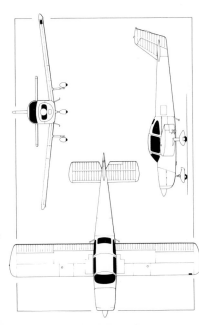

Photo and Drawing: FA-200-160

Data: FA-200-180

Power plant: One Lycoming IO-360-B1B four-cylinder piston engine (180 hp)

Wing span: 30 ft 11 in (9.42 m)
Length overall: 26 ft 2¼ in (7.98 m)
Cabin:
Length: 5 ft 8½ in (1.74 m)
Width: 3 ft 4½ in (1.03 m)
Weight empty: 1 433 lb (650 kg)
Max T-O weight (Normal category, four-seat version): 2 535 lb (1 150 kg)
Max cruising speed (75% power) at 5 000 ft (1 525 m) (Normal, four-seat version): 110 knots (127 mph; 204 km/h)
Max rate of climb at S/L (Normal, four-seat version): 760 ft (232 m)/min
Service ceiling (Normal, four-seat version): 13 700 ft (4 175 m)
Range with max fuel (Normal, four-seat version): 534 nm (615 miles; 970 km)
Accommodation: Seating for up to four persons. Shelf for 44 lb (20 kg) of baggage. Additional baggage compartment for 176 lb (80 kg). Dual controls optional

Variants:

FA-200-160. Basic version with 160 hp Lycoming O-320-D2A engine: certificated as two-seater (Aerobatic category), three-seater (Utility) or four-seater. In production

FA-200-180. Developed version, as described above: certificated as two-seater (Aerobatic category) and four-seater (Utility and Normal categories). In production

FA-203S. Experimental STOL version (one only) with leading-edge slats and full-span trailing-edge "flaperond

111

GAZUIT-VALLADEAU GAZELLE (France)

First flight 1969

Two / four-seat light aircraft

Data: GV 10-31

Power plant: One Lycoming four-cylinder piston engine (150 hp)

Wing span: 28 ft 8½ in (8.75 m)

Length overall: 21 ft 7¾ in (6.60 m)

Weight empty: 1 212 lb (550 kg)

Max T-O weight: 2 182 lb (990 kg)

Max cruising speed (75% power): 122 knots (140 mph; 225 km/h)

Max rate of climb at S/L: 787 ft (240 m) / min

Service ceiling: 14 760 ft (4 500 m)

Range: 594 nm (683 miles; 1 100 km)

Accommodation: Seating for four persons. Max permissible load on rear seat is 340 lb (154 kg). Space for 22 lb (10 kg) of baggage. Dual controls optional

Variants:

GV 10-20. Aerobatic two-seat version with 115 hp Lycoming engine. In production

GV 10-31. Four-seat version, as described above. In production. Four / five-seat version with 180 hp engine under development

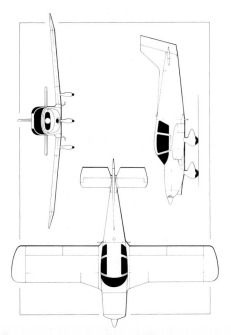

Photo: GV 10-31

113

GRUMMAN AMERICAN AA-1B TRAINER/Tr-2 and AMERICAN AVIATION YANKEE (USA)

First flights 1970/1971/1963

Two-seat light aircraft

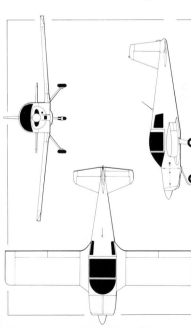

Photo: Tr-2
Drawing: AA-1
Data: AA-1B Trainer (Standard)
Power plant: One Lycoming O-235-C2C four-cylinder piston engine (108 hp)
Wing span: 24 ft 6 in (7.47 m)
Length overall: 19 ft 3 in (5.86 m)

Cabin:
Length: 4 ft 6 in (1.37 m)
Max width: 3 ft 5 in (1.04 m)
Max height: 3 ft 9¼ in (1.15 m)
Weight empty: 980 lb (445 kg)
Max T-O weight: 1 560 lb (708 kg)
Max cruising speed (75% power) at 3 000 ft (915 m): 108 knots (124 mph; 200 km/h)
Max rate of climb at S/L: 705 ft (215 m)/min
Service ceiling: 12 750 ft (3 886 m)
Range (75% power) at 3 000 ft (915 m), no reserve: 378 nm (435 miles; 700 km)
Accommodation: Seating for two persons side by side. Optional seat for child. Space for 100 lb (45 kg) of baggage aft of seats

Variants:
AA-1 Yankee. Initial production version, based on original Bede BD-1 design. Production (more than 450 by American Aviation Corpn) completed
AA-1A Trainer. Trainer version of Yankee: modified wings, some equipment changes
AA-1B Trainer. Current version of Trainer, as described above. In production by Grumman American
AA-2 American Patriot. High-performance development of AA-1, evolved by American Aviation and flown in 1970. No production
Tr-2. Dual-role advanced trainer/sporting aircraft, developed by Grumman American and based on AA-1B. In production

115

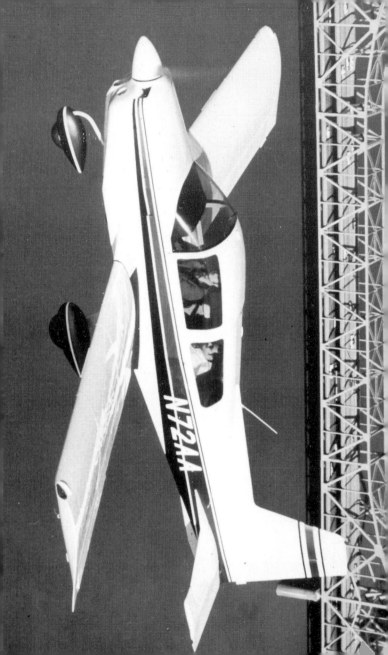

GRUMMAN AMERICAN AA-5 and TRAVELER (USA)

First Flight 1970

Four-seat light aircraft

Data: AA-5 and Traveler
Power plant: One Lycoming O-320-E2G four-cylinder piston engine (150 hp)
Wing span: 31 ft 6 in (9.60 m)
Length overall: 22 ft 0 in (6.71 m)
Cabin:
  Length: 6 ft 6 in (1.98 m)
  Max width: 3 ft 5 in (1.04 m)
  Max height: 4 ft 0¼ in (1.23 m)
Baggage space: 12 cu ft (0.34 m³)
Weight empty: 1 200 lb (544 kg)
Max T-O weight: 2 200 lb (998 kg)
Max cruising speed (75% power) at 8 500 ft (2 600 m): 122 knots (140 mph; 225 km/h)
Max rate of climb at S/L: 660 ft (201 m)/min
Service ceiling: 12 650 ft (3 855 m)
Range at max cruising speed, 45 min reserve: 390 nm (450 miles; 724 km)
Accommodation: Pilot and three passengers, in pairs. Baggage area aft of rear seats, which may be folded forward when unoccupied to increase baggage space to 41.5 cu ft (1.18 m³). Max baggage load 120 lb (54.4 kg)
Variants:
  AA-5. Basic version. Dual controls optional. In production
  Traveler. De luxe version, including as standard dual controls and much other equipment which is available optionally for the AA-5. In production

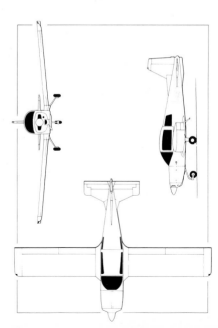

Photo and Drawing: Traveler

GRUMMAN (SCHWEIZER) AG-CAT (USA)

First flight 1957

Single-seat agricultural biplane

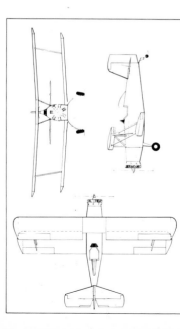

Photo: Super Ag-Cat
Drawing: Ag-Cat

Data: G-164A Super Ag-Cat
Power plant: One Pratt & Whitney R-985 (450 hp) or R-1340 (600 hp) nine-cylinder radial piston engine
Wing span: 35 ft 11 in (10.95 m)

Length overall:
R-985: 24 ft 3 in (7.39 m)
R-1340: 24 ft 3⅝ in (7.40 m)
Weight empty, equipped, spraying version:
R-985: 2 796 lb (1 268 kg)
R-1340: 3 126 lb (1 418 kg)
Max T-O Weight: 6 075 lb (2 755 kg)
Working speed:
R-985: 82.5-91 knots (95-105 mph; 153-169 km/h)
R-1340: 87-100 knots (100-115 mph; 161-185 km/h)
Max range of climb at S/L:
R-985: 580 ft (177 m)/min
R-1340: 900 ft (274 m)/min
Accommodation: Single seat in open cockpit
Equipment: Forward of cockpit is 33 cu ft (0.93 m³) or, optionally, 40 cu ft (1.13 m³) glassfibre hopper for agricultural chemicals (dry or liquid) with distributor beneath fuselage. High, low or ultra low volume spray system, with leading- or trailing-edge booms

Variants:
Ag-Cat. Initial version, type-certificated for use with 220-225 hp Continental, 240 hp Gulf Coast W-670-240, 245 hp Jacobs L-4M or L-4ME, 275-300 hp Jacobs R-755, 450 hp Pratt & Whitney R-985 or 600 hp Pratt & Whitney R-1340 engine. Production (400 by Schweizer) completed
Super Ag-Cat. Current version, as described above. In production by Schweizer

119

HAL HA-31 Mk II BASANT (SPRING) (India)

First flight 1972

Single-seat agricultural and utility aircraft

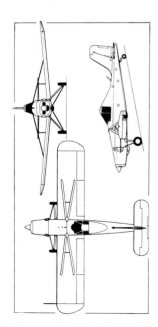

Power plant: One Lycoming IO-720-C1B eight-cylinder piston engine (400 hp)
Wing span: 39 ft 4½ in (12.00 m)
Length overall (tail down): 29 ft 6¼ in (9.00 m)
Weight empty: 2 645 lb (1 200 kg)
Max T-O weight: 5 000 lb (2 270 kg)
Max cruising speed at 8 000 ft (2 625 m), at basic operating weight of 4 300 lb (1 954 kg): 100 knots (115 mph; 185 km/h)
Max rate of climb at S/L, weight as above: 750 ft (228 m)/min
Service ceiling, weight as above: 12 500 ft (3 800 m)
Range with max fuel, no payload, weight as above: 348 nm (400 miles; 645 km)
Accommodation: Single seat. Can be used for agricultural, aerial survey, fire / patrol and cloud-seeding duties
Equipment: Glassfibre hopper, installed between engine firewall and front wall of cockpit enclosure, can carry up to 1 333 lb (605 kg) of pesticide for Normal category operation and up to 2 000 lb (907 kg) in Restricted category
Variants: Standard agricultural version, as described above; other equipment according to role. In production. Much modified from Mk I prototype

121

HAL HUL-26 PUSHPAK (India)

First flight 1958

Two-seat light aircraft

Power plant: One Continental C90-8F or Rolls-Royce Continental four-cylinder piston engine (90 hp)
Wing span: 36 ft 0 in (10.97 m)
Length overall: 21 ft 0 in (6.40 m)
Weight empty: 870 lb (395 kg)
Max T-O weight: 1 350 lb (613 kg)
Cruising speed: 61-74 knots (70-85 mph; 112-136 km/h)
Max rate of climb at S/L: 500 ft (152 m)/min
Service ceiling: 14 000 ft (4 270 m)
Range: 217 nm (250 miles; 400 km)
Accommodation: Seating for two persons side by side. Dual controls. Space for 65 lb (29.5 kg) baggage
Variants: Standard version, as described above. Production (approx 150) completed

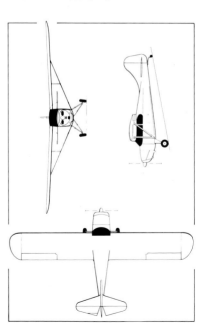

HILLER 360/UH-12 series (USA)

First flight 1948

Three-seat light helicopter

Max normal T-O weight: 2 800 lb (1 270 kg)
Max overload T-O weight (FAR 133): 3 100 lb (1 405 kg)
Max cruising speed at S/L: 78 knots (90 mph; 145 km/h)
Max rate of climb at S/L: 1 290 ft (393 m)/min
Service ceiling: 15 200 ft (4 630 m)
Range with auxiliary tanks at AUW of 2 800 lb (1 270 kg): 379 nm (437 miles; 703 km)

Accommodation: Seating for three persons. Baggage compartment behind engine, capacity 125 lb (57 kg)

Equipment: Can be adapted for agricultural operations, using dust, spray or aerosol equipment. Other optional equipment includes dual controls, stretchers, personnel hoist, cargo racks, broadcast loudspeaker and siren, external net, and load sling

Civil variants:

Model 12. Initial production version: 178 hp Franklin 6V4-178-B33 engine

Model 12A. Improved version (from 1950): new rotor blades. Later aircraft have 200 hp 6V4-200-C33 or 210 hp 6V-335-B Franklin engine

Model 12B. Generally similar to late-production Model 12A, with 200 or 210 hp Franklin engine

Model 12C. Major redesign, including all-metal rotor blades and "goldfish bowl" cockpit hood

Model 12E. Further-improved version, designated **12E-L3** with VO-540-C2B engine, as described above, and **12E-SL3** with 315 hp Lycoming TIVO-540-A2A turbocharged engine

Model E4. Available either as a kit for the 12E or as a production aircraft. Four-seater, with lengthened fuselage and sweptback stabilising surfaces

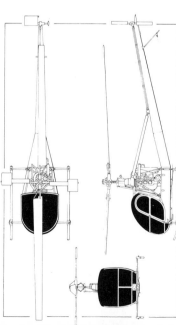

Photo and Drawing: Model 12E
Data: Hiller 12E-L3
Power plant: One Lycoming VO-540-C2B six-cylinder piston engine (305 hp)
Main rotor diameter: 35 ft 5 in (10.80 m)
Length of fuselage: 28 ft 6 in (8.69 m)
Cabin: Length: 5 ft 0 in (1.52 m)
    Max width: 4 ft 11 in (1.50 m), Max height: 4 ft 5 in (1.35 m)
Weight empty: 1 759 lb (798 kg)

125

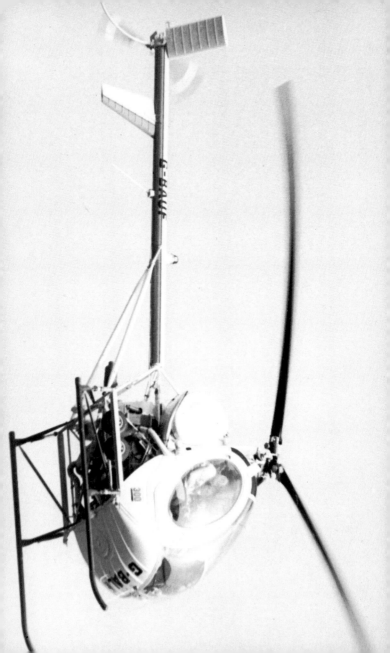

HUGHES MODEL 300 series (USA)

First flight 1956

One- to three-seat light helicopter

Data: Model 300C

Power plant: One Lycoming HIO-360-D1A four-cylinder piston engine (190 hp)

Main rotor diameter: 26 ft 10 in (8.18 m)

Length overall: 30 ft 11 in (9.42 m)

Cabin:
Length: 4 ft 7 in (1.40 m)
Max width: 4 ft 3 in (1.30 m)
Max height: 4 ft 4 in (1.32 m)

Weight empty: 1 039 lb (471 kg)

Max T-O weight: 1 900 lb (861 kg)

Max cruising speed at 5 000 ft (1 525 m): 87 knots (100 mph; 161 km/h)

Service ceiling: 12 000 ft (3 660 m)

Range with max fuel, 5 min engine warm-up, econ cruising speed of 70 knots (81 mph; 130 km/h) at 5 000 ft (1 525 m), no reserve: 202 nm (232 miles; 373 km)

Accommodation: Seating for three persons side by side

Equipment: Optional equipment includes stretchers, cargo rack, external load sling of 600 lb (272 kg) capacity, agricultural spray or dispersal kits, and dual controls

Civil variants:

Model 300 (originally Model 269B). Initial civil version: 180 hp Lycoming HIO-360-A1A engine and 25 ft 3½ in (7.71 m) main rotor. In production

Model 300C (originally Model 269C). Higher-powered version, as described above: 45 per cent increase in payload, larger-diameter main and tail rotors, lengthened tailboom, larger-area fin. In production

127

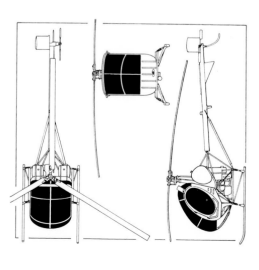

Photo: Model 300C   **Drawing**: Model 300

HUGHES MODEL 500 (USA)

First flight 1963 (OH-6)

Five-seat light helicopter

Data: Model 500

Power plant: One Allison 250-C18A turboshaft engine (317 shp, derated to 278 shp for T-O and 243 shp max continuous)

Main rotor diameter: 26 ft 4 in (8.03 m)

Length of fuselage: 23 ft 0 in (7.01 m)

Cabin:
Length: 8 ft 0 in (2.44 m)
Max width: 4 ft 6 in (1.37 m)
Max height: 4 ft 3½ in (1.31 m)

Weight empty: 1 088 lb (493 kg)

Max normal T-O weight: 2 550 lb (1 157 kg)

Max overload T-O weight: 3 000 lb (1 360 kg)

Cruising speed for max range at S/L: 117 knots (135 mph; 217 km/h)

Max rate of climb at S/L: 1 700 ft (518 m)/min

Service ceiling: 14 400 ft (4 390 m)

Range at 4 000 ft (1 220 m): 327 nm (377 miles; 606 km)

Accommodation: Pilot and four passengers or equivalent freight. Optional accommodation for seven with litter kit in use or with four in passenger compartment

Equipment: Optional equipment includes dual controls, cargo hook, hoist, litter kit and seating for four in passenger compartment

Civil variants:

Model 500: Standard civil version, as described above. In production

Model 500C. As Model 500 except for 400 shp Allison 250-C20 engine (derated to same T-O and max continuous ratings as Model 500) for improved "hot and high" performance. In production

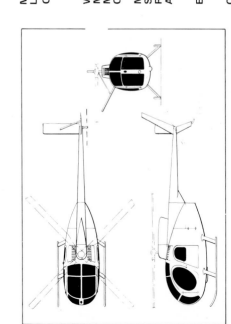

Photo: Model 500 (Kawasaki-built)
Drawing: Model 500

129

ICA-BRASOV IAR-823 (Romania)

First flight 1973

Two / five-seat light aircraft

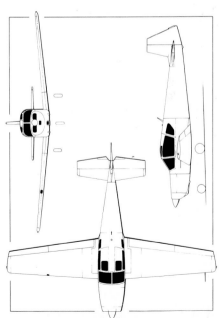

Data: Prototype (performance data estimated)
Power plant: One Lycoming IO-540-G1D5 six-cylinder piston engine (290 hp)
Wing span: 32 ft 9¾ in (10.00 m)
Length overall: 27 ft 0¼ in (8.24 m)
Weight empty:
Aerobatic 1 940 lb (880 kg)
Utility 1 984 lb (900 kg)
Max T-O weight:
Aerobatic 2 614 lb (1 186 kg)
Utility 3 042 lb (1 380 kg)
Max cruising speed (75% power) at 5 750 ft (1 750 m), at 3 086 lb (1 400 kg) AUW: 151 knots (174 mph; 280 km/h)
Max rate of climb at S/L, at above AUW: 1 378 ft (420 m)/min
Service ceiling at above AUW: 19 025 ft (5 800 m)
Range, according to mission and payload: 377-728 nm (435-838 miles; 700-1 350 km)
Accommodation: Seating for two persons side by side at front of cabin, with removable bench seat at rear for up to three more people. Space at rear of cabin for 88 lb (40 kg) of baggage. Equipment and layouts can be varied for use as air taxi, executive or freight transport, ambulance, liaison or photographic aircraft. Dual controls standard in training version, optional in other versions
Variants: Under development. Standard version expected to be similar to prototype, as described above, with equipment according to role

131

ICA-BRASOV IAR-822/826/827 series (Romania)

First flight 1970

Single/two-seat agricultural and utility aircraft

Data: IAR-827 (performance data estimated)
Power plant: One Lycoming IO-720 eight-cylinder piston engine (400 hp)
Wing span: 47 ft 6¾ in (14.50 m)
Length overall: 33 ft 9½ in (10.30 m)
Weight empty: 2 800 lb (1 270 kg)
Chemical payload (for 2 hr mission): 1 807 lb (820 kg)
Max payload: more than 1 984 lb (900 kg)
Max T-O weight: 5 202 lb (2 360 kg)
Cruising speed (agricultural version, with equipment, at max T-O weight): 97 knots (112 mph; 180 km/h)
Max rate of climb at S/L (version and AUW as above): 689 ft (210 m)/min
Operational ceiling (version and AUW as above): 8 200 ft (2 500 m)
Service ceiling: 9 850 ft (3 000 m)
Max range (standard version, no external agricultural equipment, at 3 306 lb; 1 500 kg AUW): 323 nm (372 miles; 600 km)
Accommodation: Single seat
Variants:

IAR-822. Initial single-seat version of mixed wood and metal construction. In production
IAR-822B. Tandem two-seat version of IAR-822 for training, glider towing and simulated agricultural operations. In production
IAR-826. As IAR-822 but of all-metal construction. In production
IAR-827. Enlarged and developed version of IAR-826, with more powerful engine and increased payload. In production

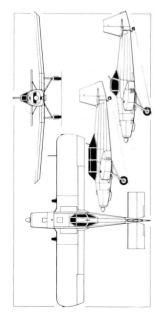

Photo: IAR-826
Drawing: IAR-822, with added side view of IAR-822B (centre)

133

First flight 1950

Two-seat light aircraft

Data: Alpavia Jodel D.117A

Power plant: One Continental C90-14F four-cylinder piston engine (95 hp)

Wing span: 26 ft 11½ in (8.22 m)

Length overall: 21 ft 4 in (6.50 m)

Weight empty: 760 lb (345 kg)

Max T-O weight: 1 323 lb (600 kg)

Max cruising speed: 105 knots (121 mph; 195 km/h)

Max rate of climb at S/L: 787 ft (240 m)/min

Service ceiling: 16 400 ft (5 000 m)

Range with max fuel, 20 min reserves: 631 nm (727 miles; 1 170 km)

Accommodation: Side-by-side seats for two persons

*Major production variants:

D.11 (2 Jodel-built prototypes), **D.111** (11 pre-production aircraft), **D.112** (562 factory-built in France by Wassmer). SAN 10, Valladeau 50 and other companies. Others built or sold in kit form in Switzerland, West Germany and Sweden), **D.117** (SAN version, 225 built). **D.117A** (Alpavia version, 10 built), **D.119D** (Valladeau version, 10 built), **D.119OS Compostela** (Aerodifusion version of D.119), **D.120 Paris-Nice** (Wassmer versions. 350 built), **D.127** (EAC version, 4 built).

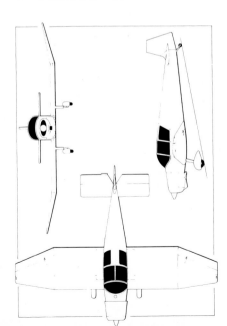

Photo: D.112
Drawing: D.11

*Many other versions built by amateur constructors (notably D.119 with 90 hp Continental engine) or by manufacturers, in France and elsewhere; these differ individually in power plant, landing gear, equipment or other details

JODEL DR.100 and CENTRE EST AMBASSADEUR/SICILE series (France)

Max rate of climb at S/L: 590 ft (180 m)/min

Range at econ cruising speed, standard fuel (DR.1051MM1 with 105 hp Potez engine): approx 564 nm (650 miles; 1 050 km)

Accommodation: Normal accommodation for three persons. Rear bench seat can accommodate two persons whose combined weight does not exceed 308 lb (140 kg). Dual controls standard

Variants:

DR.100A. Initial three-seat version with 90 hp Continental C90 engine. Production (10 by Centre Est Aéronautique, 59 by SAN) completed

DR.105A Ambassadeur. Version developed by CEA with 100 hp Continental O-200-A engine. Production (21 by SAN) completed

DR.1050 and DR.1051 Ambassadeur. Main production versions of DR.105A, with O-200-A and 105 hp Potez 4 E 20 engine respectively. Production (362 by SAN, 148 by CEA) completed

DR.1050 and DR.1051 Sicile. Improved versions of above, with O-200-A and Potez 4 E 20 engine respectively. Production (114 by CEA) completed

DR.1050M and D.1051M Excellence. Modifications of DR.1050 and DR.1051 Ambassadeur respectively, with sweptback fin and rudder and one-piece elevator. Production (38 by SAN) completed

DR.1050MM1 and DR.1051MM1 Sicile Record. Modifications of DR.1050 and DR.1051 Sicile respectively, with sweptback fin and rudder and one-piece elevator. Production (58 by CEA) completed

First flights 1958/1958/1963

Three/four-seat light aircraft

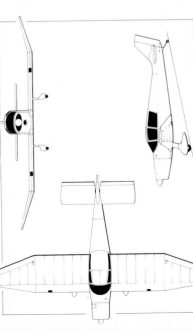

Drawing: Sicile

Photo: DR.1050 Ambassadeur

Data: Centre Est DR.1050MM1 Sicile Record

Power plant: One Continental O-200-A four-cylinder piston engine (100 hp)

Wing span: 28 ft 7½ in (8.72 m)

Length overall: 20 ft 10 in (6.35 m)

Weight empty: 882-970 lb (400-440 kg)

Max T-O weight: 1 720 lb (780 kg)

Max cruising speed (75% power) at 6 560 ft (2 000 m): 116 knots (133 mph; 215 km/h)

KAMOV Ka-26 (USSR)
NATO code name *Hoodlum*

First flight 1965

Light general-purpose helicopter

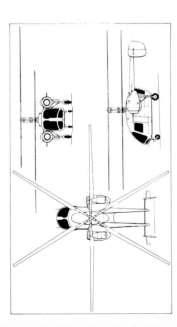

Power plant: Two Vedeneev M-14V-26 nine-cylinder radial piston engines (each 325 hp)

Rotor diameter (each): 42 ft 8 in (13.00 m)

Length of fuselage: 25 ft 5 in (7.75 m)

Passenger pod:
Length, floor level: 6 ft 0 in (1.83 m)
Width, floor level: 4 ft 1¼ in (1.25 m)
Headroom: 4 ft 7 in (1.40 m)

Operating weight, empty (stripped): 4 300 lb (1 950 kg)

Max payload:
Transport: 1 985 lb (900 kg)
Agricultural duster: 2 348 lb (1 065 kg)
Agricultural sprayer: 1 985 lb (900 kg)
With cargo platform: 2 348 lb (1 065 kg)
Flying crane: 2 425 lb (1 100 kg)

Normal T-O weight:
Transport: 6 780 lb (3 076 kg)
Agricultural: 6 570 lb (2 980 kg)

Max T-O weight: 7 165 lb (3 250 kg)

Max cruising speed: 81 knots (93 mph; 150 km/h)

Agricultural operating speed range: 16-62 knots (19-71 mph; 30-115 km/h)

Service ceiling: 9 840 ft (3 000 m)

Range with 7 passengers, 30 min fuel reserve: 215 nm (248 miles; 400 km)

Max range with auxiliary tanks: 647 nm (745 miles; 1 200 km)

Accommodation: Seating for one or two pilots and up to seven passengers. Alternative layouts for freight carrying (internal or sling cargo), ambulance, rescue, geophysical survey, aerial survey, agricultural and firefighting duties. As an ambulance can accommodate two stretcher patients, two sitting casualties and a medical attendant. For agricultural work the chemical hopper has a capacity of 1 985 lb (900 kg) and dust-spreader or spraybars are fitted. A 330 lb (150 kg) capacity winch is fitted in rescue role.

Variants: Standard version is fitted with mission pod or other equipment according to role. In production

KAWASAKI KH-4 (Japan)

First flight 1962

Light general-purpose helicopter

Power plant: One Lycoming TVO-435-D1A six-cylinder piston engine (270 hp)
Main rotor diameter: 37 ft 1½ in (11.32 m)
Length of fuselage: 32 ft 7¼ in (9.93 m)
Weight empty: 1 890 lb (857 kg)
Max T-O weight: 2 850 lb (1 292 kg)
Cruising speed: 76 knots (87 mph; 140 km/h)
Max rate of climb at S/L: 850 ft (260 m)/min
Service ceiling: 18 500 ft (5 640 m)
Range with max fuel: 186 nm (214 miles; 345 km)
Accommodation: Seating for four persons. Kits are available to equip the aircraft with agricultural dusting and spray gear, cargo sling or stretchers
Variants: Standard version (developed from Bell 47G-3B), as described above: equipment according to role. In production

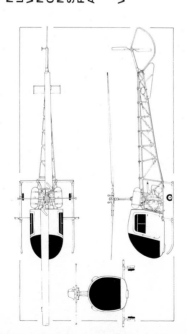

L-40 META-SOKOL (Czechoslovakia)

First flight 1954

Three/four-seat light aircraft

Data: M 332-powered version (performance data based on 115 hp rating)

Power plant: One M 332 four-cylinder piston engine (115 hp basic, 140 hp for 5 min with supercharging)

Wing span without tip-tanks: 32 ft 9¾ in (10.00 m)

Length overall: 24 ft 8¾ in (7.54 m)

Weight empty: 1 146 lb (520 kg)

Max T-O weight: 2 028 lb (920 kg)

Max cruising speed: 112 knots (129 mph; 208 km/h)

Max rate of climb at S/L: 630 ft (192 m)/min

Service ceiling: 14 765 ft (4 500 m)

Max range: 458 nm (528 miles; 850 km)

Accommodation: Seating for four persons. Baggage compartment accessible from cabin

Variants: Initial version was three-seater; major four-seat production versions had either 105 hp Walter Minor 4-III or 115/140 hp M 332 engine, as described above. Late-production aircraft had provision for wingtip auxiliary fuel tanks

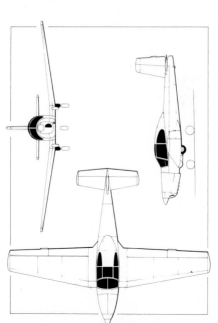

143

LAKE LA-4 / BUCCANEER (USA)

First flight 1959

Four-seat amphibian

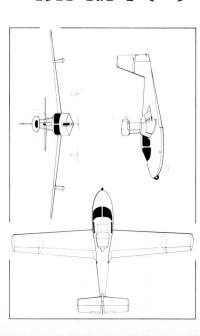

Photo: LA-4-200 Buccaneer
Drawing: LA-4

Data: LA-4-200 Buccaneer
Power plant: One Lycoming IO-360-A1B four-cylinder piston engine (200 hp)
Wing span: 38 ft 0 in (11.58 m)
Length overall: 24 ft 11 in (7.60 m)

Cabin:
Length: 5 ft 2 in (1.57 m)
Max width: 3 ft 5½ in (1.05 m)
Max height: 3 ft 11½ in (1.32 m)
Volume approx: 60 cu ft (1.70 m³)
Baggage hold: 8.5 cu ft (0.24 m³)
Weight empty, equipped: 1 600 lb (726 kg)
Max T-O weight: 2 690 lb (1 220 kg)
Max cruising speed (75% power) at 8 000 ft (2 440 m):
130 knots (150 mph; 241 km/h)
Max rate of climb at S/L: 1 200 ft (366 m)/min
Service ceiling: 14 700 ft (4 480 m)
Range with max fuel, at max cruising speed, with reserve:
564 nm (650 miles; 1 046 km)
Max range with max fuel, with reserve: 735 nm (847 miles; 1 363 km)

Accommodation: Seating for pilot and three passengers. Dual controls. Baggage compartment, capacity 200 lb (90.7 kg), aft of cabin

Variants:
LA-4. Initial version, developed by Lake from Colonial C-2 Skimmer IV via LA-4P prototype: 180 hp Lycoming O-360-A1A engine
LA-4A. As LA-4 but with shorter bow. Two only, preceding LA-4
LA-4S. Seaplane version of LA-4 without wheeled landing gear and associated equipment
LA-4T. Similar to LA-4 except for 180 hp Lycoming O-360-A1D engine and Rajay turbocharger
LA-4-200 Buccaneer. More powerful current version of LA-4, as described above. In production

LAVERDA / AEROMERE FALCO series (Italy)

First flight 1955

Two-seat light aircraft

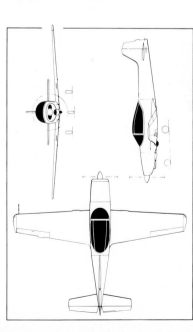

Photo and Drawing: F.8.L Super Falco

Data: F.8.L Super Falco Series IV

Power plant: One Lycoming O-320-B3B four-cylinder piston engine (160 hp)

Wing span: 26 ft 3 in (8.00 m)

Length overall: 21 ft 4 in (6.50 m)

Cabin:
  Length: 4 ft 7 in (1.40 m)
  Width: 3 ft 5 in (1.05 m)
  Height: 3 ft 4 in (1.02 m)

Weight empty: 1 212 lb (550 kg)

Max T-O weight: 1 808 lb (820 kg)

Max cruising speed at 5 000 ft (1 525 m): 156 knots (180 mph; 290 km/h)

Max rate of climb at S/L (fixed-pitch propeller): 984 ft (300 m)/min

Service ceiling: 19 700 ft (6 000 m)

Range with max fuel: 755 nm (870 miles; 1 400 km)

Accommodation: Seating for two persons side by side. Dual controls standard. Baggage locker behind seats. Provision for fitting seat for a child of not more than 90 lb (40 kg) weight in baggage space

Variants:

F.8.L Series I. Initial production version: 135 hp Lycoming O-290-D2B engine. Production (10 by Aviamilano) completed

F.8.L Series II. Development of Series I: 150 hp Lycoming O-320-A engine. Production (20 by Aviamilano) completed

F.8.L America. Basically similar to Series II but modified to CAR Pt 3 requirements

F.8.L Super Falco Series IV. Generally similar to F.8.L America but 160 hp engine, as described above. Production (20 by Laverda) completed

147

LET L-200 MORAVA (Czechoslovakia)

First flight 1957

Four/five-seat light business aircraft

Data: L-200D
Power plant: Two M 337 six-cylinder piston engines (each 210 hp)
Wing span: 40 ft 4½ in (12.31 m)
Length overall: 28 ft 3 in (8.61 m)
Weight empty, standard equipment: 2 932 lb (1 330 kg)
Max T-O weight: 4 300 lb (1 950 kg)
Econ cruising speed at 8 200 ft (2 500 m): 138 knots (159 mph; 256 km/h)
Max rate of climb at S/L: 1 260 ft (384 m)/min
Service ceiling: 18 700 ft (5 700 m)
Range with max fuel: 923 nm (1 063 miles; 1 710 km)
Accommodation: Seating for four/five persons. Dual controls. Passenger seats removable to convert into ambulance carrying pilot, two stretchers and a medical attendant. Baggage capacity 297 lb (135 kg)

Variants:
L-200. Initial version: 160 hp Walter Minor 6-III engines
L-200A. Developed version: 210 hp M 337 engines, two-blade propellers. Production (160) completed
L-200D. As L-200A, but three-blade propellers, strengthened landing gear, improved hydraulics and electronics. Production (approx 300) completed

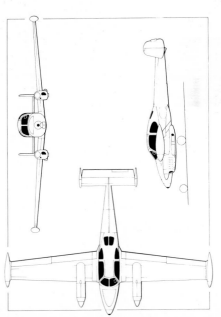

Photo: L-200D

149

LET Z-37 CMELÁK (BUMBLE-BEE) (Czechoslovakia)

First flight 1963

Single / two-seat agricultural aircraft

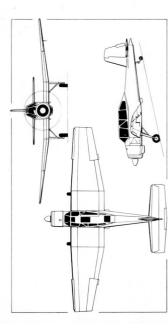

Photo: Z-37
Drawing: Z-237

Data: Standard Z-37
Power plant: One M 462 RF nine-cylinder radial piston engine (315 hp)
Wing span: 40 ft 1¼ in (12.22 m)

151

Length overall: 28 ft 0½ in (8.55 m)
Weight empty, standard equipment, without agricultural equipment: 2 295 lb (1 043 kg)
Max chemicals: 1 323 lb (600 kg)
Max T-O weight:
freight version 3 855 lb (1 750 kg)
agricultural version 4 080 lb (1 850 kg)
Cruising speed at 4 920 ft (1 500 m):
freight version 99 knots (114 mph; 183 km/h)
agricultural version 92 knots (106 mph; 170 km/h)
Max rate of climb at S/L:
freight version 925 ft (282 m)/min
agricultural version 728 ft (222 m)/min
Service ceiling (freight version): 13 125 ft (4 000 m)
Range, with reserves for 1 hour's flying, plus 10% (freight version): 345 nm (398 miles; 640 km)
Accommodation: Seat for pilot in cockpit forward of hopper. One auxiliary seat behind hopper for mechanic or loader
Equipment: Hopper for 143 Imp gallons (650 litres) of spray or 1 323 lb (600 kg) of dust. Spray system and distributor for dry chemicals interchangeable. Total volume available for chemical hopper or cargo 63.5 cu ft (1.8 m³)

Variants:
Z-37. Basic version, as described above. In production
Z-37-A. Improved version (from 1971) with stronger and more corrosion-resistant airframe and other changes. In production
Z-237. Tandem two-seat version for training pilots for agricultural flying. In production

MAULE M-4 series (USA)

Four-seat light aircraft

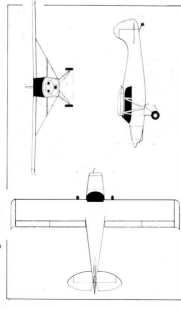

Drawing: Rocket
Photo: M-5-220C Lunar Rocket

Data: M-4 Rocket
Power plant: One Continental IO-360-A six-cylinder piston engine (210 hp)
Wing span, cambered tips: 30 ft 10 in (9.40 m)
Length overall: 22 ft 0 in (6.71 m)
Cabin:
Length: 8 ft 4 in (2.54 m)
Max width: 3 ft 6½ in (1.08 m)
Max height: 3 ft 10½ in (1.18 m)

Weight empty: 1 220 lb (553 kg)
Max T-O weight: 2 300 lb (1 043 kg)
Max cruising speed, 75% power at optimum altitude: 143 knots (165 mph; 265 km/h)
Max rate of climb at S/L: 1 250 ft (380 m)/min
Service ceiling: 18 000 ft (5 500 m)
Range with max standard fuel: 590 nm (680 miles; 1 090 km)

Accommodation: Seating for four persons, in pairs. Dual controls. Space for 100 lb (45 kg) baggage aft of rear bench seat. Provision for removing passenger seats to enable the aircraft to be used for cargo, ambulance or agricultural duties. Double cargo door standard

Variants:

M-4 Jetasen. Basic model: 145 hp Continental O-300-A four-cylinder engine, non-cambered wingtips, optional double cargo door. In production

Cuauhtemoc M-1. "Hot and high" version of basic M-4, built in Mexico by SADASA: 180 hp Lycoming O-360-A four-cylinder engine

M-4 Astro-Rocket. De luxe version of Jetasen: 180 hp Franklin 6A-335-B1A engine, cambered wingtips, double cargo door as standard. In production

M-4 Rocket. More powerful version of Astro-Rocket, as described above. In production

M-4 Strata-Rocket. Similar to Rocket but with 220 hp Franklin 6A-350-C1 engine. In production

M-5-220C Lunar Rocket. Development of Strata-Rocket as STOL cargo aircraft, with 30 per cent increase in flap area, enlarged tail surfaces, four cabin doors. In production

153

MBB BO 105 (Germany)

First flight 1966
Light general-purpose helicopter

Data: BO 105C

Power plant: Two Allison 250-C18 (317 shp 250-C20 (400 shp turboshaft engines

Main rotor diameter: 32 ft 2¾ in (9.82 m)

Length, excl main rotor: 28 ft 0½ in (8.55 m)

Weight empty: 2 447 lb (1 110 kg)

Max T-O weight: 5 070 lb (2 300 kg)

Max cruising speed at S / L (Allison 250-C20 engines), at normal T-O weight: 125 knots (144 mph; 232 km/h)

Max rate of climb at S / L, engines and weight as above: 1 870 ft (570 m)/min

Service ceiling, engines and weight as above: 16 500 ft (5 030 m)

Range with standard fuel, no reserves, engines and weight as above:
337 nm (388 miles; 625 km)

Max range with auxiliary tanks, engines and weight as above:
571 nm (658 miles; 1 060 km)

Accommodation: Pilot and passenger on front seats. Removable dual controls. Rear bench seat for three or four persons. Rear seat removable for carrying cargo or two stretchers. Entire rear fuselage aft of seats and under power-plant available as freight and baggage space

Equipment: Provision for rescue winch, agricultural equipment or cargo hook

Variants:

BO 105C. Standard civil version, as described above.

BO 105M. Military version. Armament on outriggers

BO 106. Basically as BO 105C, but cabin lengthened to seat seven persons

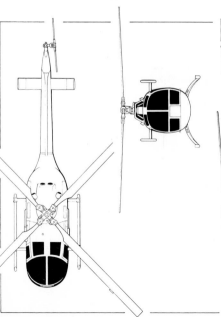
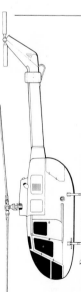

Photo and Drawing: BO 105C

155

MBB BO 209 MONSUN (MONSOON) (Germany)

First flight 1967

Two-seat light aircraft

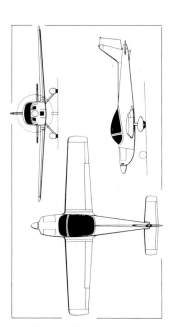

Data: BO 209-160

Power plant: One Lycoming IO-320-D1A four-cylinder piston engine (160 hp)

Wing span: 27 ft 6¾ in (8.40 m)

Length overall: 21 ft 7¾ in (6.60 m)

Cabin:
Max length: 4 ft 7 in (1.40 m)
Max width: 3 ft 3¾ in (1.01 m)
Max height: 3 ft 7¾ in (1.11 m)

Weight empty, equipped: 1 067 lb (484 kg)

Max payload: 504 lb (229 kg)

Max T-O weight: 1 807 lb (820 kg)

Max cruising speed (75% power) at 8 000 ft (2 440 m): 148 knots (170 mph) (274 km/h)

Max rate of climb at S/L: 1 180 ft (360 m)/min

Service ceiling: 18 100 ft (5 520 m)

Max range, no reserves (65% power): 647 nm (745 miles; 1 200 km)

Accommodation: Seating for pilot and one passenger side by side. Space for 110 lb (50 kg) of baggage aft of seats

Variants:

BO 209-150. 150 hp Lycoming O-320 series engine, fixed-pitch propeller

BO 209-160. 160 hp IO-320 engine, constant-speed propeller, as described above

BO 209S. Training version: non-folding wings, non-retractable nosewheel, 130 hp Rolls-Royce Continental O-240 engine

Photo and Drawing: BO 209-160

MFI / MBB (BÖLKOW) BO 208 JUNIOR (Sweden / Germany)

First flight 1958

Two-seat light aircraft

Data: MBB BO 208 C Junior
Power plant: One Rolls-Royce Continental O-200-A four-cylinder piston engine (100 hp)
Wing span: 26 ft 4 in (8.02 m)
Length overall: 19 ft 0 in (5.79 m)
Weight empty, equipped: 837 lb (380 kg)
Max T-O weight:
  Normal 1 390 lb (630 kg)
  Utility 1 320 lb (600 kg)
Max cruising speed: 111 knots (127 mph; 205 km/h)
Max rate of climb at S/L: 785 ft (240 m)/min
Service ceiling: 14 760 ft (4 500 m)
Range with max fuel: 538 nm (620 miles; 1 000 km)
Accommodation: Seating for two persons side by side. Central Y-type control column
Equipment: Optional equipment includes glider and banner towing attachment
Variants:
MFI-9 Junior. Initial Swedish (MFI) version. Production (25) completed
MFI-9 Trainer. Developed MFI-9: enlarged cabin and vertical tail surfaces, electrically-operated flaps. Production (70, including military Mili-trainers) completed
BO 208 C Junior. Designation of MFI-9 Junior after production taken over by Bölkow (later MBB) in Germany. Production (approx 200) completed

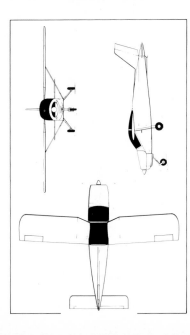

Photo and Drawing: BO 208C Junior

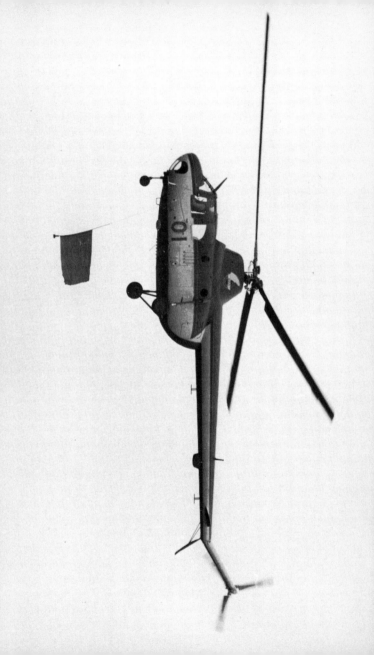

MIL Mi-1 (USSR)

First flight 1948

NATO code name *Hare*

Three-/four-seat light general-purpose helicopter

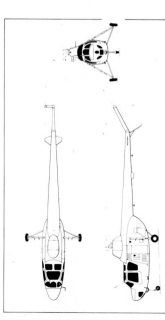

Photo and Drawing: Mi-1

Data: Mi-1NKh

Power plant: One Ivchenko AI-26V seven-cylinder piston engine (575 hp)

Main rotor diameter: 46 ft 11 in (14.30 m)

Length overall, tail rotor turning: 43 ft 6 in (13.26 m)
Length of fuselage: 39 ft 4¾ in (12.01 m)
Weight empty: 3 964 lb (1 798 kg)
Max T-O weight: 4 960 lb (2 250 kg)
Max level speed at S/L: 102 knots (118 mph; 190 km/h)
Econ cruising speed: 76 knots (87 mph; 140 km/h)
Service ceiling: 9 850 ft (3 000 m)
Range with max fuel: 205 nm (236 miles; 380 km)
Range with 330 lb (150 kg) payload: 188 nm (217 miles; 350 km)

Accommodation: Seating for pilot and three passengers. Alternative accommodation for two stretcher panniers and attendant in ambulance version, mail-carrying containers in postal version, or large external hopper and dust spreader or spraybars in agricultural version. The chemical payload for the agricultural hopper is 880 lb (400 kg)

Variants:

Mi-1. Standard four-seat version

Mi-1NKh. Utility freight/ambulance/mail/agricultural version, as described above

Mi-1T. Three-seat version of Mi-1: some equipment changes

Mi-1U. Dual-control trainer version

Mi-1 Moskvich. Refined version for Aeroflot, with hydraulic controls and equipment/instrumentation changes

SM-1. Basic designation of Polish licence-built versions, which included SM-1W (pilot and three passengers), SM-1WS (ambulance), SM-1WZ (agricultural) and SM-1WSZ (dual-control trainer)

First flight 1952

NATO code name *Hound*

General-purpose medium helicopter

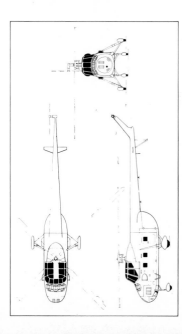

Photo and Drawing: Mi-4P

MIL Mi-4 (USSR)

Data: Mi-4P

Power plant: One Shvetsov ASh-82V eighteen-cylinder radial piston engine (1 700 hp)

Main rotor diameter: 68 ft 11 in (21.00 m)

Length of fuselage: 55 ft 1 in (16.80 m)

Cabin volume: 565 cu ft (16.0 m³)

Max payload: 3 835 lb (1 740 kg)

Normal T-O weight: 16 535 lb (7 500 kg)

Max T-O weight: 17 200 lb (7 800 kg)

Max level speed at 4 920 ft (1 500 m): 113 knots (130 mph; 210 km/h)

Econ cruising speed: 86 knots (99 mph; 160 km/h)

Service ceiling: 18 000 ft (5 500 m)

Range with 11 passengers and 220 lb (100 kg) baggage: 134 nm (155 miles; 250 km)

Range with 8 passengers and 220 lb (100 kg) baggage: 217 nm (250 miles; 400 km)

Accommodation: Flight crew of two and 8-11 passengers or equivalent freight. Aft of cabin are a toilet, wardrobe and compartment for 220 lb (100 kg) of baggage. Ambulance version carries eight stretchers and attendant

Variants:

Mi-4. Basic military and civil freight version: circular cabin windows, under-fuselage gondola (military) and (on freighter) double clamshell rear loading doors

Mi-4P. Passenger or ambulance version, as described above: square cabin windows, no ventral gondola

Mi-4S. Agricultural version, with 2 200 lb (1 000 kg) or 352 Imp gallon (1 600 litre) chemical container in cabin, and appropriate dispersal equipment

163

NAVION series (USA)

Four / five-seat light aircraft

Data: Navion Model H

Power plant: One Continental IO-520-B six-cylinder piston engine (285 hp)

Wing span: 34 ft 9 in (10.59 m)

Length overall: 27 ft 6 in (8.38 m)

Weight empty: 1 945 lb (882 kg)

Max T-O weight: 3 315 lb (1 504 kg)

Normal cruising speed: 163 knots (188 mph; 302 km/h)

Max rate of climb at S/L: 1 375 ft (420 m)/min

Service ceiling: 21 500 ft (6 550 m)

Range with max fuel: 1 454 nm (1 675 miles; 2 695 km)

Accommodation: Seating for pilot and four passengers. Dual controls. Passenger seats removable for freight carrying. Baggage space aft of rear seat, capacity 180 lb (82 kg)

Variants:

NA-145 Navion. Initial four-seat civil version: 185 hp Continental engine. Production (1 110 by North American in 1946-47) completed

Navion 205. Standard Ryan version: 205 hp Continental E185-3 engine. Production (more than 1 000 in 1948-50) completed

Navion Super 260. Higher-powered Ryan version: 260 hp Lycoming GO-435-C2 engine. Production (1950-51) completed

Rangemaster. Improved five-seat version, developed by Navion Aircraft Co in 1960: 260 hp Continental IO-470-H engine. Later production aircraft fitted with smaller, re-contoured fin and rudder

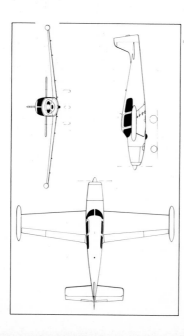

Photo and Drawing: Rangemaster

NIPPER series (Belgium / UK)

First flight 1957

Single-seat ultra-light aircraft

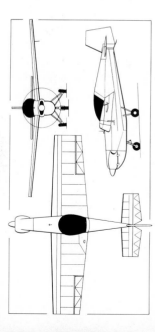

Photo: Nipper Mk III
Drawing: Nipper Srs IV

Data: Nipper Mk III
Power plant: One Rollason Ardem X four-cylinder piston engine (45 hp)
Wing span (without tip-tanks): 19 ft 8 in (6.00 m)
Wing span (with tip-tanks): 20 ft 6 in (6.25 m)

Length overall: 15 ft 0 in (4.56 m)
Weight empty: 465 lb (210 kg)
Max T-O weight:
Aerobatic: 685 lb (310 kg)
Normal: 750 lb (340 kg)
Max cruising speed (75% power) at S/L:
without tip-tanks: 81 knots (93 mph; 150 km/h)
Max rate of climb at S/L: 650 ft (198 m)/min
Service ceiling: 12 000 ft (3 660 m)
Range with max internal fuel, 30 min reserve: 173 nm (200 miles; 320 km)
Range with tip-tanks: 390 nm (450 miles; 720 km)
Accommodation: Single seat. Small baggage space aft of seat
Variants:

Nipper Mk I. Initial version, built by Avions Fairey (Belgium) with 40 hp Pollmann HEPU engine in 1959
Nipper Mk II. As Mk I except for 45 hp Stark Stamo 1400A engine; built by Avions Fairey and other Belgian manufacturers from 1959
Nipper Mk III. First UK-built version, as described above, with optional wingtip tanks. Originally built by Slingsby under contract to Nipper Aircraft; and was also available in kit form for amateur construction. Manufacture suspended, though assistance to homebuilders continues
Nipper Mk IIIA. As Mk III, but with option of 55 hp 1 600 cc Ardem engine. Status as Mk III
Nipper Srs IV. Projected version. Lengthened nose

167

PARTENAVIA P.64 and P.66 OSCAR series (Italy)

First flight 1965

Two- to four-seat light aircraft

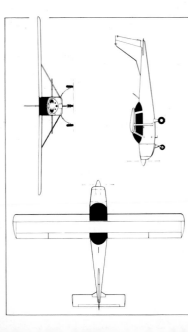

Photo and Drawing: P.64B Oscar

Data: P.64B Oscar-180
Power plant: One Lycoming O-360-A1A four-cylinder piston engine (180 hp)
Wing span: 32 ft 9¼ in (9.99 m)
Length overall: 23 ft 8¾ in (7.23 m)
Weight empty: 1 477 lb (670 kg)
Max T-O weight: fixed-pitch prop: 2 425 lb (1 100 kg)
variable-pitch prop: 2 546 lb (1 155 kg)

Max cruising speed (75% power) at 7 000 ft (2 150 m): 129 knots (149 mph; 240 km/h)
Max rate of climb at S/L: 984 ft (300 m)/min
Service ceiling: 16 400 ft (5 000 m)
Endurance (75% power): 4 hr 30 min
Accommodation: Seating for four persons. Dual controls. Baggage space aft of rear seats

Variants:

P.64 Oscar Standard. Initial four-seat basic version: constant-speed propeller, blind-flying instrumentation, radio, VOR, ADF, optional glassfibre wheel fairings

P.64 Oscar Club. As above but fixed-pitch propeller, VHF radio

P.64 Oscar Cargo. Similar to Standard but fixed-pitch propeller, reinforced floor, wider rear door for freight

P.64B Oscar-180 (originally Oscar-B). Development of P.64, as described above: stepped-down rear fuselage, panoramic rear cabin window. In production

RSA 200 Falcon. Designation of Oscar 180 built by AFIC in South Africa. Production suspended

P.64B Oscar-200. Similar to Oscar-180 but 200 hp Lycoming IO-360-A1B engine, variable-pitch propeller. In production

P.66 Oscar. Two-seat version of P.64: 115 hp Lycoming O-235-C1B engine

P.66B Oscar-100. Current two-seat version, developed from P.66: same design improvements as Oscar-180. In production

P.66B Oscar-150. Three-seater, similar to Oscar-100 but 150 hp Lycoming O-320-E2A engine. In production

169

PIPER PA-18 SUPER CUB 150 (USA)

First flight 1949

Two-seat light aircraft

Length overall: 22 ft 7 in (6.88 m)
Baggage compartment: 18 cu ft (0.51 m³)
Weight empty (Normal category): 930 lb (422 kg)
Max T-O weight (Normal category): 1 750 lb (794 kg)
Max cruising speed (75% power), Normal category: 100 knots (115 mph; 185 km/h)
Max rate of climb at S/L (Normal category): 960 ft (293 m)/min
Service ceiling (Normal category): 19 000 ft (5 795 m)
Range with max fuel and max payload (Normal category): 399 nm (460 miles; 735 km)
Accommodation: Seating for two persons in tandem. Dual controls. Rear seat quickly removable for cargo carrying. Baggage compartment aft of rear seat, capacity 50 lb (22 kg)
Equipment: Equipment may be installed for spraying, dusting, fertilising, etc

Civil variants:
PA-18-95 and PA-18-105. Initial versions (1949) with, respectively, 90 hp Continental C90-12F and 108 hp Lycoming O-235 engine. Successor to pre-war E-2/J-2/J-3/J-4 Cub series and post-war PA-11 Cub Special
PA-18-135. 1952: 135 hp Lycoming O-290-D2 engine
PA-18-150. 1955: 150 hp Lycoming O-320 engine; available in standard or de luxe form. Production, with successive detail refinements, continues. Designations **PA-18A-150** and **PA-18S** apply to agricultural and twin-float versions respectively

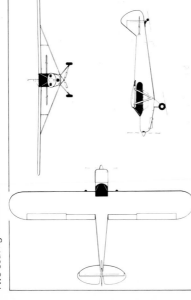

Photo and Drawing: PA-18-150

Data: Standard Super Cub 150 (landplane)
Power plant: One Lycoming O-320 four-cylinder piston engine (150 hp)
Wing span: 35 ft 2½ in (10.73 m)

171

PIPER PA-22 TRI-PACER / COLT / CARIBBEAN (USA)

First flights 1951 / 1961 / 1958

Two-seat (Colt) or four-seat light aircraft

Data: Colt PA-22-108 (standard model)

Power plant: One Lycoming O-235-C1B four-cylinder piston engine (108 hp)

Wing span: 30 ft 0 in (9.14 m)

Length overall: 20 ft 0 in (6.10 m)

Weight empty: 940 lb (426 kg)

Max T-O weight: 1 650 lb (748 kg)

Max cruising speed (75% power) at 7 000 ft (2 135 m): 100 knots (115 mph; 185 km/h)

Max rate of climb at S/L: 610 ft (186 m)/min

Service ceiling: 12 000 ft (3 660 m)

Range with standard fuel: 281 nm (324 miles; 554 km)

Range with 36 US gallons (136 litres) max optional fuel at 7 000 ft (2 135 m): 599 nm (690 miles; 1 110 km)

Accommodation: Seating for two persons side by side

Variants:

Tri-Pacer. Tricycle-gear version of earlier PA-20 Pacer; introduced 1951 as four-seat **PA-22-125** and **PA-22-135** with 125 or 135 hp Lycoming O-290-D2 engine, the latter being standard from 1953. Followed 1955 by **PA-22-150** (150 hp Lycoming O-320) and 1957 by **PA-22-160** (160 hp Lycoming O-320-B)

Caribbean. Introduced 1958 as simplified, lower-cost counterpart of PA-22-150 Tri-Pacer

Colt. 1961: side-by-side two-seat version of Tri-Pacer, with 108 hp Lycoming O-235-C1B engine

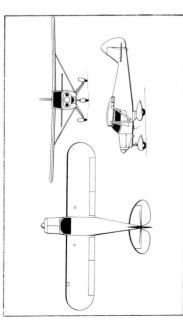

Photo: Tri-Pacer (160 hp)
Drawing: Colt

173

PIPER PA-23 APACHE (USA)

First flight 1952

Four / five-seat light aircraft

Length overall: 27 ft 7 in (8.41 m)
Weight empty (standard): 2 735 lb (1 240 kg)
Max T-O weight: 4 800 lb (2 177 kg)
Max cruising speed (75% power) at 7 000 ft (2 135 m): 166 knots (191 mph; 307 km/h)
Max rate of climb at S/L: 1 450 ft (442 m)/min
Service ceiling: 17 200 ft (5 240 m)
Range with max fuel (75% power): 851 nm (980 miles; 1 575 km)
Range with max fuel (55% power): 1 029 nm (1 185 miles; 1 905 km)

Accommodation: Standard seating for four persons, in pairs. Provision for fitting an extra seat at rear of cabin. Dual controls. Compartment for 200 lb (91 kg) baggage. With only the front two seats installed, there is 80 cu ft (2.27 m³) of space for a stretcher, camera or cargo

Variants:

Apache A. Initial version, introduced 1954 as four-seat **PA-23-150** with 150 hp Lycoming O-320 engines. Annual detail refinements in **Apache B to E** (1955-58)

Apache F (originally PA-23-160). 1959: 160 hp Lycoming O-320-B engines

Apache G. 1960: optional fifth seat, extra cabin windows; 1961 **Apache H** similar

Apache 235 (PA-23-235). Replaced Apache H 1962: 235 hp Lycoming O-540-B1A5 engines, four / five seats, swept fin and rudder, all-moving tailplane, as described above

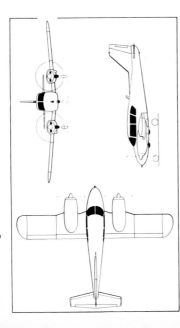

Photo: Apache G
Drawing: Apache 235

Data: PA-23-235 Apache 235
Power plant: Two Lycoming O-540-B1A5 six-cylinder piston engines (each 235 hp)
Wing span: 37 ft 1¾ in (11.33 m)

PIPER PA-23-250 AZTEC (USA)

First flight 1959

Six-seat light aircraft

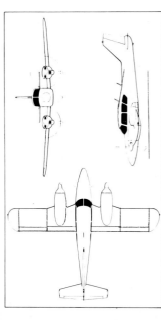

Photo: Aztec E

Data: Aztec E
Power plant: Two Lycoming IO-540-C4B5 six-cylinder piston engines (each 250 hp)
Wing span: 37 ft 2½ in (11.34 m)
Length overall: 31 ft 2¾ in (9.52 m)
Max cargo space, incl baggage compartments: 122 cu ft (3.45 m³)
Weight empty (standard): 3 042 lb (1 379 kg)
Max T-O weight: 5 200 lb (2 360 kg)

Normal cruising speed at 4 000 ft (1 220 m): 182 knots (210 mph; 338 km/h)
Long-range cruising speed at 10 200 ft (3 110 m): 169 knots (195 mph; 314 km/h)
Max rate of climb at S/L: 1 490 ft (455 m)/min
Absolute ceiling: 21 100 ft (6 430 m)
Range with max fuel:
Normal cruising speed 720 nm (830 miles; 1 335 km)
Long-range cruising speed 1 050 nm (1 210 miles; 1 947 km)

Accommodation: Seating for six persons, in pairs. Dual controls standard. Centre and rear pairs of passenger seats removable to provide space for stretcher, survey camera or up to 1 600 lb (725 kg) freight. Baggage compartments at rear of cabin and in nose, each with capacity of 150 lb (68 kg)

Civil variants:
Aztec A. Initial five-seat version (1959), developed from PA-23 Apache: 250 hp Lycoming O-540-A1D5 engines
Aztec B. 1962: six-seater, longer nose
Aztec C. 1964: 250 hp Lycoming IO-540-C4B5 engines in redesigned nacelles, modified landing gear
Aztec D. 1968: new instrument panel and other interior improvements
Aztec E. 1970: longer nose, added automatic flight capability. In production
Turbo Aztec. Designation for aircraft with AiResearch turbocharging system, first introduced 1964 with Turbo Aztec C. Current E model (in production) has 250 hp Lycoming TIO-540-C1A engines fitted with this system

177

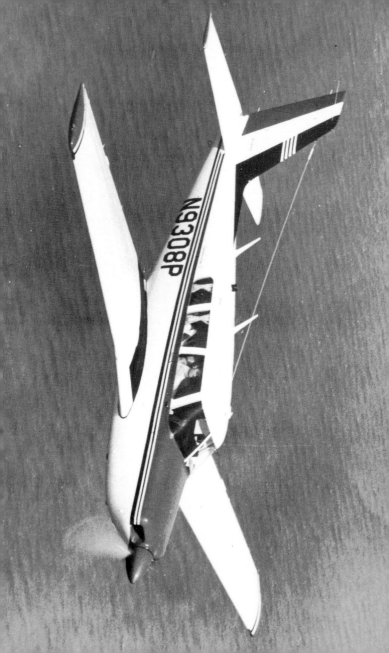

PIPER PA-24-260 COMANCHE (USA)

First flight 1956

Four- to six-seat light aircraft

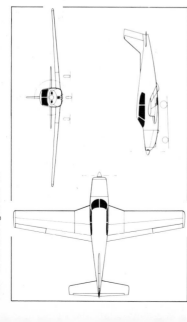

Photo: Turbo Comanche C
Drawing: PA-24-250

Data: Comanche C
Power plant: One Lycoming IO-540 six-cylinder piston engine (260 hp)
Wing span: 36 ft 0 in (10.97 m)
Length overall: 25 ft 0 in (7.62 m)
Cabin length: 9 ft 4 in (2.84 m)

Weight empty (standard model): 1 773 lb (804 kg)
Max T-O weight: 3 200 lb (1 451 kg)
Max cruising speed (75% power) at 6 300 ft (1 920 m): 161 knots (185 mph; 298 km/h)
Max rate of climb at S/L: 1 320 ft (402 m)/min
Service ceiling: 19 500 ft (5 945 m)
Range (75% power) with standard fuel at 6 300 ft (1 920 m): 638 nm (735 miles; 1 180 km)
Range (65% power) with optional fuel at 10 500 ft (3 200 m): 1 063 nm (1 225 miles; 1 970 km)
Accommodation: Standard version has seating for four persons, in pairs. Seating for two extra persons optional. All seats other than front two are quickly removable to provide space for stretcher, camera or freight. Dual controls standard. Baggage compartment, capacity 250 lb (113 kg), aft of cabin

Variants:

PA-24-180. Initial four-seat version (1957): 180 hp Lycoming O-360-A1A engine
PA-24-250. 1958: 250 hp Lycoming O-540-A1A5 engine
PA-24-400. 1963: strengthened airframe, larger tail surfaces, all-moving tailplane, 400 hp Lycoming IO-720 engine, three-blade propeller
PA-24-260 Comanche. 1964: 260 hp Lycoming O-540-E or IO-540-D engine. Optional fifth/sixth seats from 1966 **Comanche B**; current version (in production) is **Comanche C**, as described above
Turbo Comanche C. As standard Comanche C but with Rajay turbocharging system; introduced 1970. In production

PIPER PA-25 and PA-36 PAWNEE (USA)

Single-seat agricultural aircraft

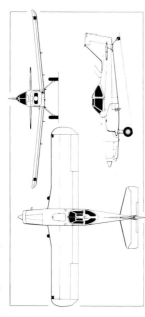

Photo: Pawnee C
Drawing: PA-36 Pawnee Brave

Data: PA-36 Pawnee Brave
Power plant: One Teledyne Continental Tiara 6-285 six-cylinder piston engine (285 hp)
Wing span: 39 ft 0 in (11.89 m)
Length overall: 27 ft 4¼ in (8.34 m)
Cockpit width: 3 ft 2 in (0.97 m)
Weight empty:
  standard 2 050 lb (930 kg)
  sprayer 2 170 lb (984 kg)

Max T-O weight:
  Normal category 3 900 lb (1 769 kg)
  Restricted category 4 400 lb (1 996 kg)
Typical working speed: 117 knots (135 mph; 217 km/h)
Accommodation: Single seat in enclosed cockpit
Equipment: Standard equipment includes a non-corrosive hopper/tank of translucent glassfibre-reinforced plastics, installed forward of cockpit. Optional hoppers of either 30 cu ft (0.85 m³) capacity, containing 225 US gallons (852 litres), or 38 cu ft (1.08 m³) capacity, containing 275 US gallons (1 041 litres). The latter has a maximum capacity for dry chemicals of 1 900 lb (862 kg). Venturi-type dry material spreaders of stainless steel or aluminium available. Spray system comprises easily-removable wind-driven spray pump and 1½ in diameter spraybooms equipped with 60 nozzles

Variants:
PA-25-150. Initial version (1959): 150 hp Lycoming O-320 engine
PA-25-235. 1962: 235 hp Lycoming O-540-B2B5 engine
Pawnee B. 1965: improved PA-25-235 with larger hopper, improved dispersal gear
Pawnee C. 1966: oleo shock-absorbers and other airframe improvements, optional 260 hp Lycoming O-540-E from 1968. In production
PA-36 Pawnee Brave (originally Pawnee II). Larger than PA-25 Pawnee, with cantilever wings, sweptback fin and rudder, as described above. Introduced December 1970: in production

181

PIPER PA-28 CHEROKEE and CHEROKEE ARROW (USA,

First flight 1960

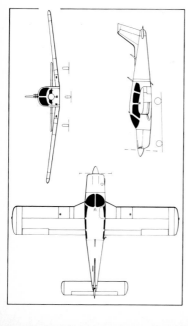

Photo: Cherokee Arrow
Drawing: Cherokee Arrow II

Data: Cherokee Arrow II
Power plant: One Lycoming IO-360-C1C four-cylinder piston engine (200 hp)
Wing span: 32 ft 0 in (9.75 m)
Length overall: 24 ft 7¼ in (7.50 m)
Weight empty, equipped: 1 517 lb (688 kg)
Max T-O weight: 2 650 lb (1 202 kg)
Max cruising speed (75% power) at optimum altitude: 143 knots (165 mph; 266 km/h)
Max rate of climb at S/L: 900 ft (274 m)/min

Service ceiling: 15 000 ft (4 575 m)
Cruising range (75% power), at optimum altitude and econ speed: 642 nm (740 miles; 1 191 km)
Accommodation: Seating for four persons, in pairs. Dual controls. Baggage compartment aft of cabin with capacity of 200 lb (90.7 kg). Rear seats removable to provide cargo space. Provision for carrying stretcher

Variants:

PA-28-150 **Cherokee C** (1961-67), PA-28-160 **Cherokee C** (1961-67), PA-28-180 **Cherokee C** (1962-67), PA-28-235 **Cherokee 235** (1963-72); subsequent refinements as **Cherokee 235B** 1966, **235C** 1968, **235D** 1970 and **235E** 1971). PA-28-140 **Cherokee 140** (1964-68); optional kit to convert to four-seat and 150 hp engine as **Cherokee 140-4**), PA-28-180/200 **Cherokee Arrow** (1967-71; initially as PA-28-180R), PA-28-200R **Arrow** (from 1969; both PA-28-180R and 200R becoming PA-28-200 in 1970; renamed **Cherokee Arrow 200B** 1971), PA-28-180 **Cherokee D** (1968-72; subsequently refined as **Cherokee 180E** 1970 and **180F** 1971), PA-28-140B **Cherokee 140B** (1969-72; subsequent refinements in 1970 to **Cherokee 140C** and 1971 **140D**), **Cherokee Flite Liner** (1971), **Cherokee Cruiser 2 + 2** (1972; replaced Cherokee 140 as standard model 1973, in production), PA-28-200 **Cherokee Arrow II** (1972; supersedes Cherokee Arrow, in production), PA-28-180 **Cherokee Challenger** (1972; supersedes Cherokee 180, in production), PA-28-235 **Cherokee Charger** (1972; supersedes Cherokee 235, in production)

PIPER PA-30 and PA-39 TWIN COMANCHE (USA)

First flight 1962

Four- to six-seat light private and business aircraft

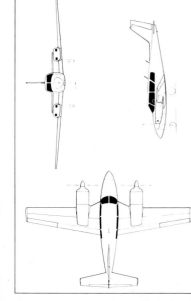

Photo: Twin Comanche C/R

Data: PA-39 Twin Comanche C/R
Power plant: Two Lycoming IO-320-B1A four-cylinder piston engines (each 160 hp)
Wing span: standard: 36 ft 0 in (10.97 m)
over tip-tanks: 36 ft 9½ in (11.22 m)
Length overall: 25 ft 2 in (7.67 m)
Baggage compartment volume: 20 cu ft (0.57 m³)
Weight empty (standard): 2 270 lb (1 029 kg)

Normal max T-O weight: 3 600 lb (1 633 kg)
Max T-O weight with tip-tanks: 3 725 lb (1 690 kg)
Normal cruising speed: 172 knots (198 mph; 319 km/h)
Max rate of climb at S/L: 1 460 ft (445 m)/min
Service ceiling: 20 000 ft (6 100 m)
Range with max standard fuel:
Normal cruising speed 720 nm (830 miles; 1 335 km)
L-range cruising speed 1 042 nm (1 200 miles; 1 930 km)
Accommodation: Seating for four persons, in pairs, in standard version. Seating for two extra persons optional. Dual controls standard. Baggage compartment capacity 250 lb (113 kg). Rear seats removable for stretcher or cargo

Variants:

PA-30. Initial four-seat version (1963): 160 hp Lycoming IO-320-B engines

PA-30B Twin Comanche B. 1965: optional fifth and sixth seats, extra cabin windows. Built in Standard, Custom and Sportsman models with equipment and instrumentation variations

PA-30C Twin Comanche C. 1 968: cabin refinements. Superseded from 1971 by PA-39 Series

PA-30 Turbo Twin Comanche B and C. As PA-30B and PA-30C above, but IO-320-C1A engines, Rajay turbocharging system, wingtip tanks as standard. Superseded from 1971 by PA-39 series

PA-39 Twin Comanche C/R. 1971: counter-rotating propellers. Available in same Standard, Custom and Sportsman versions as Twin Comanche C, which it has superseded. In production

PA-39 Turbo Twin Comanche C/R. As PA-30 Turbo versions but counter-rotating propellers. In production

185

PIPER PA-32 CHEROKEE SIX (USA)

First flight 1963

Six / seven-seat light aircraft

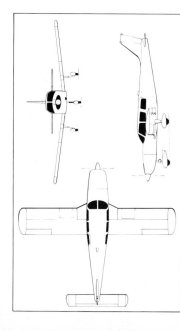

Photo: Cherokee SIX 300

Data: Cherokee SIX 300
Power plant: One Lycoming IO-540-K six-cylinder piston engine (300 hp)
Wing span: 32 ft 9½ in (9.99 m)
Length overall: 27 ft 8¾ in (8.45 m)
Cabin:
Length, panel to rear wall: 9 ft 11 in (3.02 m)
Max width: 4 ft 1 in (1.24 m)
Max height: 4 ft 0½ in (1.23 m)

Baggage compartment volume:
forward: 8 cu ft (0.23 m³)
aft: 22 cu ft (0.62 m³)
Weight empty, equipped (standard): 1 818 lb (824 kg)
Max T-O weight: 3 400 lb (1 542 kg)
Max cruising speed (75% power) at optimum altitude: 146 knots (168 mph; 270 km/h)
Max rate of climb at S/L: 1 050 ft (320 m)/min
Service ceiling: 16 250 ft (4 950 m)
Cruising range (75% power) at optimum altitude: 738 nm (850 miles; 1 368 km)
Cruising range (55% power) at optimum altitude: 894 nm (1 030 miles; 1 658 km)
Accommodation: Seating for six persons, in pairs. Optional seventh seat standard. Dual controls standard. Space for 100 lb (45 kg) baggage at rear of cabin, and another 100 lb forward. A set of four pieces of matched luggage to fit the nose baggage compartment is provided as standard. Passenger seats easily removable to provide up to 110 cu ft (3.11 m³) of cargo space inside cabin, or room for stretcher and one or two attendants

Variants:
PA-32-260 Cherokee SIX 260. Initial version (1965). Enlarged six-seat development of PA-28 Cherokee series: larger fuselage and cabin, 260 hp Lycoming O-540-E4B5 engine, strengthened landing gear, wider-span tailplane. Optional seventh seat from 1966, increased cabin space from 1969. In production
PA-32-300 Cherokee SIX 300. 1966: higher-powered version with 300 hp Lycoming IO-540-K engine; same subsequent refinements as PA-32- 260 In production

PIPER PA-31T CHEYENNE (USA)

First flight 1969

Six- to eight-seat twin-engined light aircraft

Power plant: Two United Aircraft of Canada PT6A-28 turboprop engines (each 620 shp)

Wing span over tip-tanks: 42 ft 8¾ in (13.02 m)

Length overall: 34 ft 8 in (10.57 m)

Cabin, incl flight deck and toilet:
Length: 16 ft 1 in (4.90 m)
Max width: 4 ft 3 in (1.30 m)
Max height: 4 ft 4 in (1.32 m)
Volume, incl front baggage compartment: 264 cu ft (7.48 m³)

Baggage compartments:
front: 20 cu ft (0.57 m³)
rear: 22 cu ft (0.62 m³)

Weight empty, equipped: 4 870 lb (2 209 kg)

Max T-O weight: 9 000 lb (4 082 kg)

Max cruising speed at 11 000 ft (3 350 m), at 7 600 lb (3 447 kg) AUW: 283 knots (326 km/h) (525 km/h)

Econ cruising speed at 25 000 ft (7 620 m), AUW as above: 184 knots (212 mph; 341 km/h)

Max rate of climb at S/L: 2 800 ft (853 m)/min

Service ceiling: 29 000 ft (8 840 m)

Range with max fuel, incl allowances for taxi, take-off, climb, descent and 45 min reserve: 1 350 nm (1 555 miles; 2 500 km)

Accommodation: Seating for pilot and co-pilot or passenger on flight deck, and up to 6 other passengers. Cabin layout includes toilet, refreshment centre, tables and baggage area. Baggage compartments at front and rear, each with a 200 lb (90.7 kg) capacity

Variants: One version only. Four production aircraft completed and eight ordered by spring 1974

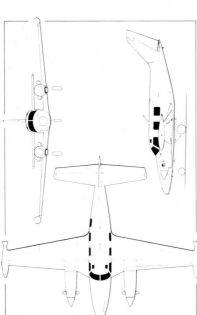

189

PIPER PA-28-151 CHEROKEE WARRIOR (USA)

Four-seat light aircraft

Power plant: One Lycoming O-320-E3D four-cylinder piston engine (150 hp)
Wing span: 35 ft 0 in (10.67 m)
Length overall: 23 ft 10 in (7.26 m)
Cabin:
Length: 9 ft 0 in (2.74 m)
Max width: 3 ft 6 in (1.07 m)
Max height: 4 ft 0 in (1.22 m)
Volume: 92 cu ft (2.61 m³)
Baggage compartment: 15 cu ft (0.42 m³)
Weight empty, equipped: 1 301 lb (590 kg)
Max T-O weight: 2 325 lb (1 054 kg)
Max cruising speed at S/L: 117 knots (135 mph; 217 km/h)
Max rate of climb at S/L: 649 ft (198 m)/min
Service ceiling: 12 700 ft (3 870 m)
Range at 75% power with max fuel: 625 nm (720 miles; 1 158 km)
Accommodation: Seating for pilot and 3 passengers. Baggage space aft of rear seats
Variants: One version only. 99 production aircraft built by Spring 1974

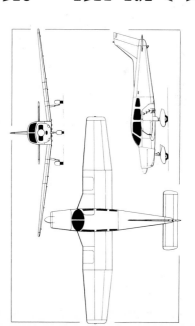

PITTS SPECIAL (USA)

First flight 1944

Single- or two-seat aerobatic biplane

Data: S-1

Power plant: One Lycoming four-cylinder piston engine (100-180 hp)

Wing span, upper: 17 ft 4 in (5.28 m)

Length overall: 15 ft 6 in (4.72 m)

Weight empty (180 hp Lycoming IO-360-B4A engine): 720 lb (326 kg)

Max T-O weight, engine as above: 1,100 lb (499 kg)

Max cruising speed at 8 000 ft (2 440 m), engine as above: 122 knots (140 mph; 225 km/h)

Max rate of climb at S/L, engine as above: 2 770 ft (844 m)/min

Service ceiling, engine as above: 18 000 ft (5 500 m)

Endurance with max fuel, no reserve, engine as above: 2 hr 48 min

Accommodation: Single seat in open cockpit

Variants:

S-1. Basic single-seat version, as described above. Plans available for amateur construction

S-2. Two-seat version (open cockpits in tandem), 180 hp Lycoming IO-360-B4A engine. Available only as factory-built aircraft. In production

S-2A. Version of S-2, of which 5 built in 1972-73 for Rotham Aerobatic Team, with 200 hp Lycoming engine. Flown during displays as single-seater, with front cockpit covered by a removable panel. Available to order

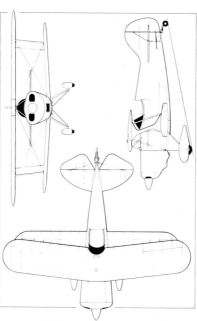

Photo and Drawing: S-1

ROBIN 400 series (France)

First flight 1972

Two- to five-seat light aircraft

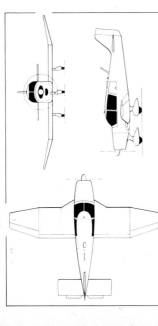

Photo: DR 400/180
Drawing: DR 400/160 Chevalier

Data: DR 400/180 Régent
Power plant: One Lycoming O-360-A four-cylinder piston engine (180 hp)
Wing span: 28 ft 7¼ in (8.72 m)
Length overall: 23 ft 6¾ in (7.18 m)
Cabin:
Length: 5 ft 3¾ in (1.62 m)
Max width: 3 ft 7¼ in (1.10 m)
Max height: 4 ft 0½ in (1.23 m)
Baggage volume: 13.75 cu ft (0.39 m³)
Weight empty, equipped: 1 301 lb (590 kg)

Max T-O weight: 2 425 lb (1 100 kg)
Max cruising speed at 8 000 ft (2 440 m): 143 knots (164 mph; 265 km/h)
Max rate of climb at S/L: 825 ft (252 m)/min
Service ceiling: 20 000 ft (6 100 m)
Range with max fuel: 793 nm (913 miles; 1 470 km)
Accommodation: Seating for four or five persons. Up to 88 lb (40 kg) of baggage can be stowed aft of rear seats when four occupants are carried

Variants:

DR 400/2+2 "2+2". Basic version: 108 hp Lycoming O-235-C2C engine. Seating for two or three adults or two adults and two children. In production, replacing earlier DR 220 "2+2" (which see) and DR 300/108

DR 400/125 Petit Prince. Three/four-seat version: similar to DR 400/2+2 but 125 hp Lycoming O-235-F2B engine. In production

DR 400/140 Major. Four-seat version: similar to DR 400/2+2 but 140 hp Lycoming O-320-E engine. In production, replacing earlier DR 340

DR 400/160 Chevalier. Four-seat version: similar to DR 400/2+2 but 160 hp Lycoming O-320-D engine, extra fuel. In production, replacing earlier DR 360 Major 160. Known as **Knight** in UK

DR 400/180 Régent. Four/five-seat version: similar to DR 400/160 but 180 hp Lycoming O-360-A engine. In production, replacing earlier DR 253 Régent and DR 380 Prince

DR 400/180R Remorqueur. As DR 400/180, but equipped for glider towing. Can also be flown as a normal four-seat tourer. In production

ROBIN DR 220 "2+2" / DR 221 DAUPHIN / DR 250 CAPITAINE (France)

First flights 1966 / 1967 / 1965

Two- to four-seat light aircraft

Data: DR 221 Dauphin

Power plant: One Lycoming O-235-C2A four-cylinder piston engine (108 / 115 hp)

Wing span: 28 ft 7¼ in (8.72 m)

Length overall: 22 ft 11½ in (7.00 m)

Weight empty, equipped: 1 047 lb (475 kg)

Max T-O weight:

Normal: 1 852 lb (840 kg)

Utility: 1 720 lb (780 kg)

Max cruising speed (75% power) at S / L, Normal category: 110 knots (127 mph; 205 km / h)

Max rate of climb at S / L, Normal category: 650 ft (198 m) / min

Service ceiling, Normal category: 12 800 ft (3 900 m)

Max range with standard fuel, Normal category: 490 nm (565 miles; 910 km)

Accommodation: Seating for two persons at front of cabin and a further two persons or baggage up to a total weight of 265 lb (120 kg) at rear. Dual controls standard

Variants:

DR 220. Initial production version: 100 hp Rolls-Royce Continental O-200-A engine. Seating for either three adults or two adults and two children

DR 220A. Improved DR 220: strengthened airframe, DR 250-type landing gear

DR 220 / 108. As DR 220 but 108 / 115 hp Lycoming O-235 engine

DR 221 Dauphin. Similar to DR 220: as described above

DR 250 Capitaine. Similar to DR 220, but 160 hp Lycoming O-320-D2A engine, seating for four adults. Can be used as glider tug

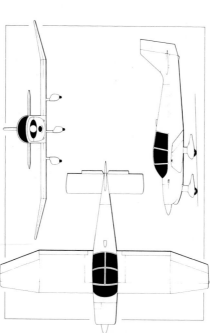

Photo: DR 221 Dauphin
Drawing: DR 220

197

ROBIN HR 100 series (France)

First flight 1969

Four- or five-seat light aircraft

Data: HR 100/210F Royal

Power plant: One Continental IO-360-D six-cylinder piston engine (210 hp)

Wing span: 29 ft 9½ in (9.08 m)

Length overall: 24 ft 3 in (7.39 m)

Weight empty: 1 565 lb (710 kg)

Max T-O weight: 2 755 lb (1 250 kg)

Max cruising speed (75% power) at 8 000 ft (2 440 m): 146 knots (168 mph; 270 km/h)

Max rate of climb at S/L: 1 000 ft (305 m)/min

Service ceiling: 16 400 ft (5 000 m)

Max range at 8 000 ft (2 440 m), 75% power: standard fuel 739 nm (850 miles; 1 370 km); auxiliary fuel 1 457 nm (1 675 miles; 2 700 km)

Accommodation: Seating for four persons. Baggage space aft of rear seats

Variants:

HR 100/200. Initial production version: 200 hp Lycoming IO-360-A1D6 engine, fixed landing gear. Production (approx. 30) completed

HR 100/210F Royal. Current (F for fixed landing gear) version, as described above. In production

HR 100/210R Royal. Current version, as HR 100/210F except for retractable landing gear. In production

HR 100/Tiara. Development of HR 100/210R, first flown 1972: redesigned wings and vertical tail, retractable landing gear, 320 hp Teledyne Continental Tiara 6-320 engine, seating for five persons. In production

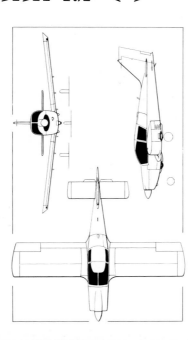

Photo and Drawing: HR 100/Tiara

199

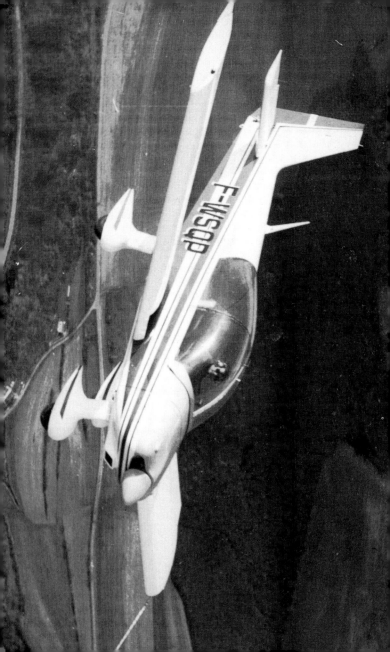

ROBIN HR 200 series (France)

First flight 1971

Two-seat fully-aerobatic light aircraft

Data: HR 200 / 100 Club
Power plant: One Lycoming O-235-C1C four-cylinder piston engine (100 hp)
Wing span: 27 ft 4 in (8.33 m)
Length overall: 21 ft 9½ in (6.64 m)
Cabin:
Max width: 3 ft 6 in (1.06 m)
Weight empty, equipped: 1 113 lb (505 kg)
Max T-O weight: 1 675 lb (760 kg)
Max cruising speed (75% power) at S/L: 116 knots (133 mph; 215 km/h)
Service ceiling: 12 950 ft (3 950 m)
Max range: 582 nm (671 miles; 1 080 km)
Accommodation: Pilot and passenger side by side. Room for 55 lb (25 kg) of baggage at rear of cabin
Variants:
HR 200 / 100 Club. Basic version, as described above. In production
HR 200 / 125 Club. 125 hp O-235 engine. In production
HR 200 / 160 Acrobin. Aerobatic version: 160 hp Lycoming IO-320-D engine. In production

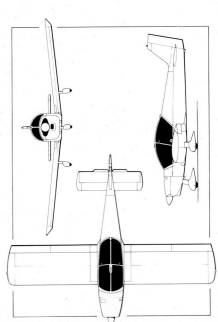

Photo: HR 200 Club

ROCKWELL COMMANDER 112 (USA)

First flight 1970

Four-seat light aircraft

Data: Model 112

Power plant: One Lycoming IO-360-C1D6 four-cylinder piston engine (200 hp)

Wing span: 32 ft 10¾ in (10.03 m)

Length overall: 25 ft 0 in (7.62 m)

Cabin:
Length: 9 ft 7½ in (2.93 m)
Max width: 3 ft 11 in (1.19 m)
Max height: 4 ft 1 in (1.24 m)

Baggage compartment: 21 cu ft (0.59 m³)

Weight empty: 1 530 lb (694 kg)

Max T-O weight: 2 550 lb (1 157 kg)

Max cruising speed (75% power) at 7 500 ft (2 285 m): 152 knots (175 mph; 281 km/h)

Max rate of climb at S/L: 1 000 ft (305 m)/min

Service ceiling: 17 000 ft (5 180 m)

Range with max fuel, no reserves: 981 nm (1 130 miles; 1 818 km)

Accommodation: Seating for pilot and three passengers, in pairs. Compartment for 200 lb (90.7 kg) of baggage

Variants:

Model 112. Initial version, as described above: retractable tricycle landing gear. In production

Model 111A. Generally similar to Model 112, but 180 hp Lycoming O-360-A1G6 engine, non-retractable tricycle landing gear. Development aircraft only.

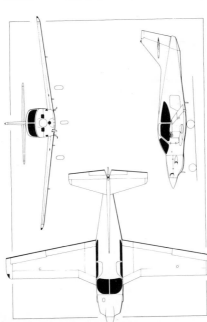

Photo and Drawing: Model 112

203

First flight 1948

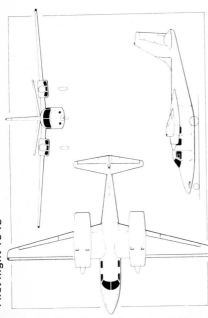

ROCKWELL COMMANDER / AERO COMMANDER series (piston-engined) (USA)

Max T-O weight: 6 750 lb (3 062 kg)
Max cruising speed (75% power) at 9 000 ft (2 745 m): 176 knots (203 mph; 326 km/h)
Max rate of climb at S/L: 1 340 ft (408 m)/min
Service ceiling: 19 400 ft (5 913 m)
Range with standard fuel at 9 000 ft (2 745 m) at 178 knots (205 mph; 330 km/h), 45 min reserves: 693 nm (798 miles; 1 525 km)

Accommodation: Standard Shrike Commander has seating for four persons, in pairs. Dual controls. Optional seating layouts for up to seven persons. Passenger furnishings can be removed for freight-carrying. Compartment for 500 lb (227 kg) of baggage. Esquire has standard seating for pilot and five passengers; standard equipment includes stereo units, foldaway desk, beverage consoles and drawers

Variants:
Aero Commander 520 (approx 150 built), **Aero Commander 560, Aero Commander 560A** (150 built), **Aero Commander 680 Super** (295 built), **Aero Commander 560E** (70 built), **Aero Commander 500** (95 built), **Aero Commander 680E, Aero Commander 720 Alti-Cruiser** (13 built). **Aero Commander 500A and 500B** (Latter version redesignated 500U, now known as **Shrike Commander**). **Aero Commander 560F** (1960 model), **Aero Commander 680F and 680FP, Grand Commander 680F/L and 680FP/L, Courser Commander, Courser-Liner, Shrike Commander and Shrike Commander Esquire** (current name, since 1967, of former Aero Commander 500B/500U. Both in production). **Commander 685** (in production)

Photo and Drawing: Shrike Commander

Data: Shrike Commander
Power plant: Two Lycoming IO-540-E1B5 six-cylinder piston engines (each 290 hp)
Wing span: 49 ft 0½ in (14.95 m)
Length overall: 36 ft 9¾ in (11.22 m)
Cabin:
Length: 10 ft 7½ in (3.24 m). Max width: 4 ft 4 in (1.32 m). Max height: 4 ft 5 in (1.35 m). Volume: 177 cu ft (5.01 m³)
Weight empty, equipped: 4 608 lb (2 090 kg)

ROCKWELL THRUSH COMMANDER (USA)

First flight 1968

Single-seat agricultural aircraft

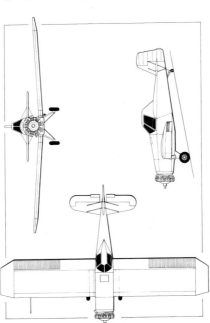

Power plant: One Pratt & Whitney R-1340-AN-1 nine-cylinder radial piston engine (600 hp)
Wing span: 44 ft 5 in (13.54 m)
Length overall: 29 ft 4 ½ in (8.95 m)
Weight empty: 3 700 lb (1 678 kg)
Max T-O weight: 6 900 lb (3 130 kg)
Cruising speed (70% power): 107.5 knots (124 mph; 200 km/h)
Max rate of climb at S/L: 900 ft (274 m)/min
Service ceiling: 15 000 ft (4 570 m)
Ferry range (at 50% power): 408 nm (470 miles; 756 km)
Accommodation: Single seat. Hopper forward of cockpit with capacity of 53 cu ft (1.50 m³) able to contain up to 400 US gallons (1 514 litres) of liquid or 3 280 lb (1 487 kg) of dry chemicals
Equipment: Standard equipment includes Universal spray system. Optional equipment includes Ag Commander high-volume spreader with micro-adjust calibrator, agitator installation and extra-high-density spray configuration with 70 nozzles installed
Variants: Standard version, as described above. In production

ROCKWELL TURBO COMMANDER (USA)

First flight 1964

Light transport

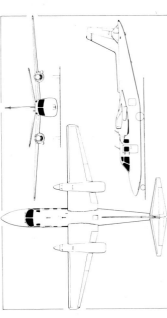

Photo: Turbo Commander 681B

Data: Turbo Commander 681B
Power plant: Two AiResearch TPE 331-43BL turboprop engines (each 605 ehp)
Wing span: 44 ft 0¾ in (13.43 m)
Length overall: 42 ft 11¾ in (13.10 m)

Cabin dimensions: As Shrike Commander
Weight empty: 5 647 lb (2 561 kg)
Max T-O weight: 9 400 lb (4 265 kg)
Max cruising speed: 241 knots (278 mph; 447 km/h)
Max rate of climb at S/L: 2 007 ft (612 m)/min
Service ceiling: 25 600 ft (7 800 m)
Cruising range with standard fuel at 21 000 ft (6 400 m) at 221 knots (254 mph; 409 km/h) TAS, with 45 min reserves: 922 nm (1 062 miles; 1 709 km)
Cruising range with max fuel, conditions as above: 1 141 nm (1 315 miles; 2 116 km)
Absolute range with max fuel, conditions as above: 1 294 nm (1 491 miles; 2 400 km)
Accommodation: Standard seating for eight persons. Optional seating for up to nine persons. Baggage compartment aft of rear pressure bulkhead, capacity 500 lb (227 kg)
Variants:

Turbo Commander. Initial production version, basically a slightly-modified Grand Commander with 605 ehp AiResearch TPE 331-43 turboprop engines and increased fuel

Turbo Commander 681B. Developed version, as described above; airframe of Courser Commander (except for shorter-span wings) and TPE 331-43BL engines. Originally known as **Turbo II Commander** and later, briefly, as **Hawk Commander.** In production

Turbo Commander 690. Pressurised 7/11-seat business transport. Airframe generally similar to 681B but engines (700 ehp TPE 331-5-251K turboprops) mounted farther outboard than 681B and drive larger-diameter propellers. In production

209

First flight 1951

ROLLASON (DRUINE) D.31 TURBULENT (UK/France)

Single-seat ultra-light aircraft

Data: D.31 Turbulent
Power plant: One Rollason Ardem 4CO2 Mk IV (45 hp) or Mk V (55 hp) four-cylinder piston engine
Wing span: 21 ft 7 in (6.58 m)
Length overall: 17 ft 6 in (5.33 m)
Weight empty: 395 lb (179 kg)
Max T-O weight: 620 lb (281 kg)
Max cruising speed (45 hp): 87 knots (100 mph; 161 km/h)
Max rate of climb at S/L (45 hp): 450 ft (137 m)/min
Service ceiling (45 hp): 9 000 ft (2 740 m)
Range with max fuel, normal allowances (45 hp): 217 nm (250 miles; 400 km)
Accommodation: Single seat in open cockpit. Baggage locker aft of seat, capacity 25 lb (11.5 kg)
Variants:

D.3. Initial (French) version: 25 hp modified Volkswagen engine

Turbulent D. German-built version (by Stark): 45 hp Stark Stamo 1400 engine, fully-transparent cockpit canopy

D.31. Standard Rollason-built version, as described above Some early aircraft had 30 hp Ardem or Porsche engines

D.31A. Rollason-developed version: improved wing main spar, 45 hp Ardem Mk X engine, max T-O weight of 700 lb (316 kg)

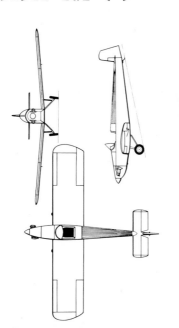

Photo and Drawing: D.31

ROLLASON (DRUINE) D.62 CONDOR (UK)

First flight 1961

Two-seat light aircraft

Data: D.62B Condor
Power plant: One Rolls-Royce Continental O-200-A four-
cylinder piston engine (100 hp)
Wing span: 27 ft 6 in (8.38 m)
Length overall: 22 ft 6 in (6.86 m)
Weight empty: 920 lb (417 kg)
Max T-O weight: 1 475 lb (670 kg)
Max cruising speed: 100 knots (115 mph; 185 km/h)
Max rate of climb at S/L: 610 ft (185m)/min
Service ceiling: 12 000 ft (3 650 m)
**Range with max fuel and max payload, normal allowan-
ces:** 285 nm (328 miles; 528 km)
Accommodation: Pilot and passenger side by side. Baggage
shelf at rear of cabin

Variants:

D.62A. Pre-production version. Production (2) completed
D.62B. Standard version, as described above.
D.62C. 130 hp Rolls-Royce Continental O-240 engine.
Specially equipped for glider towing, with wingtip end-
plates, larger wheels, raised cockpit canopy.

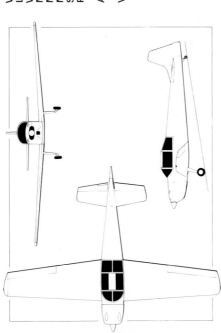

Photo and Drawing: D.62B

213

SAN JODEL D.140 MOUSQUETAIRE (MUSKETEER) and ABEILLE (BEE) and D.150 MASCARET (TIDAL WAVE) (France)

First flights 1956 / 1965 / 1962

Two / four / five-seat light aircraft

Max cruising speed (75% power) at 7 000 ft (2 300 m): 129 knots (149 mph; 240 km/h)

Max rate of climb at S/L: 750 ft (230 m)/min

Service ceiling: 16 400 ft (5 000 m)

Range with max fuel: 755 miles (870 miles; 1 400 km)

Accommodation: Seating for four or five persons. Dual controls optional. Large baggage locker, capacity 25 cu ft (0.70 m³), can carry stretcher in ambulance role. Small locker, capacity 10 cu ft (0.28 m³), for baggage, auxiliary fuel tank or emergency equipment. Max baggage capacity 210 lb (96 kg). With five passengers 44 lb (20 kg)

Variants:

D.140A Mousquetaire. Initial four-seat version, with non-swept fin and rudder. Production completed

D.140B Mousquetaire II. As D.140A except modified

D.140C Mousquetaire III. As D.140B except sweptback fin and rudder. Production completed

D.140 E Mousquetaire IV. As D.140C except for increases in flap and vertical tail area, one-piece elevator and modified ailerons. Production completed. Total Mousquetaire production (all versions) 193

D.140R Abeille. Development of D.140E for glider towing, with fully-transparent bulged canopy. 22 built

D.150 Mascaret. Two-seat version with 100 hp Continental O-200-A engine and sweptback fin and rudder: 63 built, including D.150A

D.150A Mascaret. As D.150 except for 105 hp Potez 4 E 20 engine

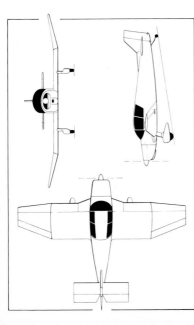

Photo and Drawing: D.150 Mascaret

Data: D.140E Mousquetaire IV

Power plant: One Lycoming O-360-A2A four-cylinder piston engine (180 hp)

Wing span: 33 ft 8¼ in (10.27 m)

Length overall: 25 ft 11¾ in (7.92 m)

Weight empty: 1 367 lb (620 kg)

Max T-O weight: 2 645 lb (1 200 kg)

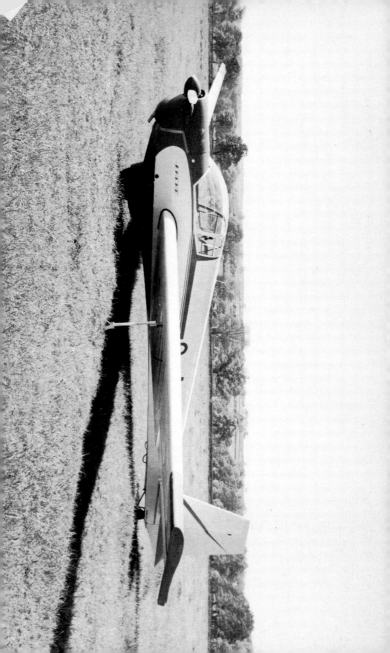

SCHEIBE FALKE (FALCON) (Germany)

First flight 1964(?)

Two-seat powered sailplane

Data: SF-25B

Power plant: One Stamo MS 1500 four-stroke piston engine (45 hp)

Wing span: 50 ft 2½ in (15.30 m)

Weight empty: 739 lb (335 kg)

Max T-O weight: 1 168 lb (530 kg)

Cruising speed: 69 knots (80 mph; 130 km/h)

Max rate of climb at S/L:
1 person: 500 ft (150 m)/min
2 persons: 400 ft (120 m)/min

Best glide ratio: 22

Min sinking speed (power off): 3.1 ft (0.95 m)/sec

Range: 191-218 nm (220-250 miles; 350-400 km)

Accommodation: Seating for two persons side by side. Dual controls standard

Variants:

SF-25B Falke. Basic version, as described above. Slingsby-built examples designated **T.61.** In production

SF-25C Falke. Improved SF-25B: 60 hp Sportavia-Limbach SL 1700 EA engine. In production

SF-28 Tandem-Falke. Generally similar to SF-25C, but seats in tandem. In production

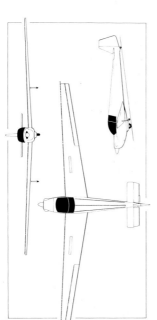

Photo and Drawing: SF-25B Falke

SCHWEIZER MODEL TSC-1 TEAL (USA)

First flight 1968

Two-seat light amphibian

Data: TSC-1A2 Teal II

Power plant: One Lycoming O-320-A3B four-cylinder piston engine (150 hp)

Wing span: 31 ft 11 in (9.73 m)

Length overall: 23 ft 7 in (7.19 m)

Weight empty: 1 435 lb (651 kg)

Max T-O weight: 2 200 lb (998 kg)

Max cruising speed at 5 000 ft (1 525 m): 101 knots (116 mph; 187 km/h) IAS

Max rate of climb at S/L: 650 ft (198 m)/min

Service ceiling: 12 000 ft (3 660 m)

Range at econ cruising speed of 96 knots (110 mph; 177 km/h) IAS, with max standard fuel and 45 min reserve: 410 nm (472 miles; 759 km)

Range at econ cruising speed, with max standard plus optional fuel and 45 min reserve: 650 nm (748 miles; 1 203 km)

Accommodation: Seating for two persons side by side. Baggage compartment behind seats, capacity 230 lb (104 kg). Optional dual controls

Variants:

TSC-1A1. Initial version. Production (15) completed

TSC-1A2 Teal II. Improved version: slotted trailing-edge flaps, new wing leading-edge fuel tanks, optional hull tank, independent retraction of tailwheel. In production

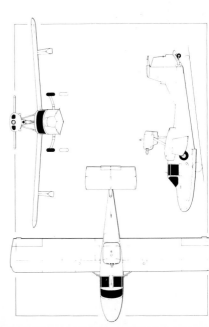

Photo: TSC-1A2 Teal II
Drawing: TSC-1A1

219

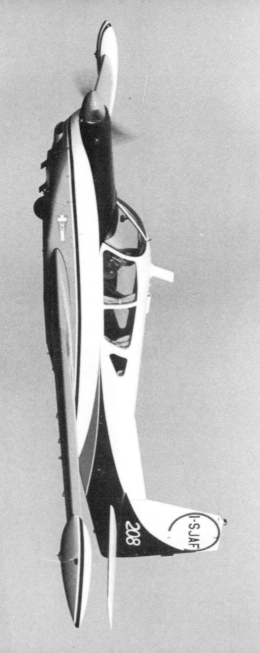

SIAI-MARCHETTI S.205/S.208 (Italy)

Four- or five-seat light aircraft

Data: S.208

Power plant: One Lycoming O-540-E4A5 six-cylinder piston engine (260 hp)

Wing span: 35 ft 7½ in (10.86 m)

Length overall: 26 ft 3 in (8.00 m)

Cabin:

Length: 5 ft 10¼ in (1.78 m)
Max width: 3 ft 8¾ in (1.14 m)
Max height: 4 ft 4 in (1.32 m)
Volume: 88.0 cu ft (2.5 m³)

Weight empty, equipped: 1 720 lb (780 kg)

Max T-O weight: 3 307 lb (1 500 kg)

Max cruising speed: 162 knots (187 mph; 300 km/h)

Range with max internal fuel: 647 nm (746 miles; 1 200 km)

Range with max fuel (incl tip-tanks): 1 085 nm (1 250 miles; 2 000 km)

Accommodation: Seating for pilot and up to four passengers. Baggage compartment aft of seats

Civil variants:

S.205-18/F. Basic four-seater: 180 hp Lycoming O-360-A1A engine, non-retractable landing gear

S.205-18/R. As -18/F but retractable landing gear

S.205-20/F. Similar to -18/F except 200 hp Lycoming IO-360-A1A engine, non-retractable landing gear

S.205-20/R. As -20/F but retractable landing gear

S.205-22/R. 220 hp Franklin 6A-350-C1 engine, retractable landing gear. Known in US as **Waco S.220 Vela**

S.208. Basic five-seater: retractable landing gear, as described above. In production

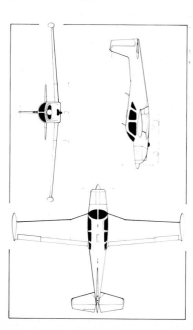

Photo and Drawing: S.208

SIAI-MARCHETTI SF.260 (Italy)

First flight 1964

Three-seat light aircraft

Power plant: One Lycoming O-540-E4A5 six-cylinder piston engine (260 hp)

Wing span over tip-tanks: 26 ft 11 ¾ in (8.25 m)

Length overall: 23 ft 0 in (7.02 m)

Weight empty, equipped: 1 543 lb (700 kg)

Max T-O weight:
Utility: 2 430 lb (1 102 kg)
Aerobatic: 2 205 lb (1 000 kg)

Max cruising speed at 10 000 ft (3 050 m), Utility: 186 knots (214 mph; 345 km/h)

Max rate of climb at S/L (Utility): 1 770 ft (540 m)/min

Service ceiling (Utility): 21 375 ft (6 500 m)

Range with max fuel (two persons, Utility): 1 107 nm (1 275 miles; 2 050 km)

Accommodation: Seating for three persons, two at front and one at rear. Two children with a combined weight not exceeding 250 lb (113 kg) may use rear seat. Baggage compartment capacity 88 lb (40 kg)

Civil variants: Standard civil version, as described above. In production

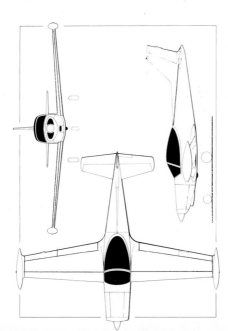

First flight 1963

Light helicopter

SILVERCRAFT SH-4 (Italy)

Data: SH-4 and SH-4A (except where indicated)
Power plant: One Franklin 6A-350-D1B six-cylinder piston engine (235 hp, derated to 170 hp)
Main rotor diameter: 29 ft 7½ in (9.03 m)
Length of fuselage, incl tailskid: 25 ft 1¼ in (7.65 m)
Cabin:

Length: 4 ft 9¾ in (1.47 m)
Max height: 4 ft 0¾ in (1.24 m)

Weight empty (SH-4): 1 142 lb (518 kg)
Max T-O weight (Normal): 1 900 lb (862 kg)
Max cruising speed: 70 knots (81 mph; 130 km/h)
Max rate of climb at S/L: 1 180 ft (360 m)/min
Service ceiling (SH-4): 15 100 ft (4 600 m)
Range with max fuel: 173 miles (200 miles; 320 km)
Accommodation: Bench seat for pilot and two passengers side by side in SH-4. Large baggage compartment. SH-4A normally flown as single-seater. Fitted with 32 ft 9½ in (10.00 m) spraybars. Max capacity of chemical tanks 53 US gallons (200 litres) up to a max weight of 441 lb (200 kg). Total weight (empty) of spray installation 82 lb (37 kg).
Optional equipment: Dual controls. Optional equipment for SH-4 only includes external cargo hook for 441 lb (200 kg) slung load; baggage container; stretcher pannier mounted externally; or agricultural equipment of the same type as fitted to the SH-4A.

Variants:
SH-4. Standard three-seat general-purpose version. In production
SH-4A. Single-seat agricultural version. In production
SH-4C. As SH-4 but with Franklin 6AS-350-D1 fitted with AiResearch exhaust-driven supercharger

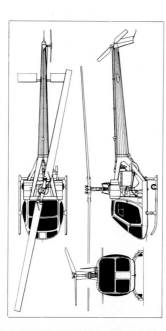

Photo: SH-4A
Drawing: SH-4

225

SOCATA GY-80 HORIZON (France)

First flight 1960

Four-seat light aircraft

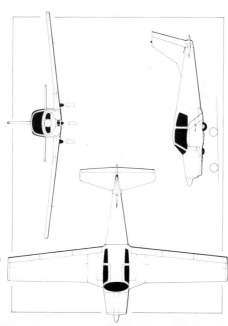

Data: Fixed-pitch propeller version.

Power plant: One Lycoming O-320-D (160 hp) or O-360-A (180 hp) four-cylinder piston engine

Wing span: 31 ft 10 in (9.70 m)
Length overall: 21 ft 9½ in (6.64 m)
Cabin:
   Length: 7 ft 2½ in (2.20 m)
   Max width: 3 ft 7 in (1.10 m)
   Max height: 4 ft 1 in (1.25 m)
Weight empty, equipped:
   160 hp: 1 334 lb (605 kg)
   180 hp: 1 360 lb (617 kg)
Max T-O weight:
   160 hp: 2 315 lb (1 050 kg)
   180 hp: 2 535 lb (1 150 kg)
Max cruising speed (75% power) at 8 200 ft (2 500 m):
   160 hp: 124 knots (143 mph; 230 km/h)
   180 hp: 130 knots (150 mph; 240 km/h)
Rate of climb at S/L:
   160 hp: 660 ft (201 m)/min
   180 hp: 850 ft (258 m)/min
Service ceiling:
   160 hp: 13 450 ft (4 100 m)
   180 hp: 14 800 ft (4 500 m)
Range with 44 Imp gallons (200 litres) fuel:
   160 hp: 512 nm (590 miles; 950 km)
   180 hp: 674 nm (777 miles; 1 250 km)
Accommodation: Seating for pilot and three passengers. Dual controls standard. Space for 88 lb (40 kg) baggage aft of rear seat

Variants: Built in four basic versions. Standard versions have 160 hp or 180 hp engine and fixed-pitch propeller, as described above; constant-speed propeller available optionally with either engine

SOCATA RALLYE series (France)

First flight 1959

Three/four-seat light aircraft

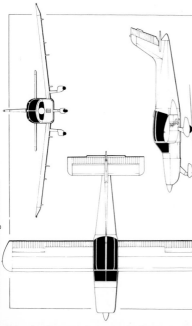

Photo: Rallye 180 GT
Drawing: Rallye 220 GT

Data: Rallye 180 GT
Power plant: One Lycoming O-360-A2A four-cylinder piston engine (180 hp)
Wing span: 31 ft 6¼ in (9.61 m)
Length overall: 23 ft 9 in (7.24 m)
Cabin: Length: 7ft 4 in (2.25 m) Width: 3 ft 8½ in (1.13 m)
Weight empty, equipped: 1 257 lb (570 kg)

Max T-O weight: 2 315 lb (1 050 kg)
Max cruising speed (75% power) at 5 000 ft (1 525 m): 121 knots (139 mph; 224 km/h)
Max rate of climb at S/L: 787 ft (240 m)/min
Service ceiling: 11 150 ft (3 400 m)
Range with max fuel: 512 nm (590 miles; 950 km)

Accommodation: Seating for four. Dual controls. Baggage space aft. Can be used as ambulance, carrying pilot, stretcher and attendant, or as glider tug or agricultural aircraft

Variants: Rallye **110 T.** Initial three-seat version (originally known as Morane-Saulnier MS 880B Rallye-Club): 100 hp Continental O-200-A engine. In production
MS **881 Rallye.** Similar to MS 880B Rallye 100 T but 105 hp Potez 4 E 20 engine. Production (12) completed
MS **883 Rallye.** Similar to MS 880B Rallye 100 T but 115 hp Lycoming engine. Production (77) completed
MS **885 Super Rallye.** Similar to Rallye 100T but 145 hp Continental O-300C engine. Production (212) completed
MS **886 Super Rallye.** Similar to MS 885 but 150 hp Lycoming O-320-E engine. Production (3) completed
MS **890 Rallye Commodore.** First four-seat version: 145 hp Continental O-300-A engine. Production completed
Rallye **125.** New (1972) four-seat version: 125 hp Lycoming O-235-F2A engine. In production
Rallye **150 GT.** Similar to MS 890 but 150 hp Lycoming O-320-E2A engine. In production
Rallye **180 GT.** Similar to 150 GT but 180 hp Lycoming O-360-A2A engine, as described above. In production
Rallye **220 GT.** Similar to 180 GT except for 220hp. Franklin 6A-350-C1 engine. In production

229

SOCATA ST 10 DIPLOMATE (France)

First flight 1967

Four-seat light aircraft

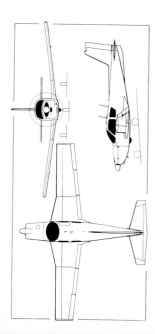

Power plant: One Lycoming IO-360-C1B four-cylinder piston engine (200 hp)

Wing span: 31 ft 9⅞ in (9.70 m)

Length overall: 23 ft 9¾ in (7.26 m)

Cabin:
Length: 7 ft 4⅝ in (2.25 m)
Max width: 3 ft 8⅞ in (1.14 m)
Max height: 4 ft 1¼ in (1.25 m)

Weight empty, equipped: 1 594 lb (723 kg)

Max T-O weight: 2 690 lb (1 220 kg)

Max cruising speed (75% power): 143 knots (165 mph; 265 km/h)

Max rate of climb at S/L: 1 003 ft (306 m)/min

Service ceiling: 16 400 ft (5 000 m)

Range with 4 persons: 746 nm (860 miles; 1 385 km)

Accommodation: Seating for four persons. Dual controls standard. Space for 154 lb (70 kg) of baggage aft of rear seat

Variants:
Standard version, as described above

First flight 1960

SPORTAVIA AVION-PLANEUR series (Germany / France)

Single- or two-seat powered sailplane

Max T-O weight:

Aerobatic: 1 333 lb (605 kg)
Utility: 1 455 lb (660 kg)

Max cruising speed at S/L: 102 knots (118 mph; 190 km/h)

Max rate of climb at S/L: 590 ft (180 m)/min

Service ceiling: 19 675 ft (6 000 m)

Range with max fuel: 410 nm (472 miles; 760 km)

Accommodation: Adjustable tandem seats for pilot and one passenger, with dual controls. Space for 22 lb (10 kg) of baggage aft of rear seat

Variants:

RF3. Initial single-seat version: 39 hp modified Volkswagen engine. Production (95 by Alpavia) completed

RF4D. Single-seat version: 40 hp Rectimo (converted VW) engine. Production (160 by Sportavia) completed, but production continued of RF4D fuselages for SFS 31 Milan

RF5. Tandem two-seat development of RF4D, as described above. Increased-span wings with folding outer panels. In production

RF5B Sperber. Improved RF5: increased wing span and area, cut-down rear fuselage, bubble-type canopy. In production

RF55. Modified RF5B, to meet FAR Pt 23: modified 60 hp Franklin 2A-120-A engine, larger fuel tank, electric fuel pump. In production

SFS 31 Milan. Hybrid version, combining RF4D fuselage, power plant and tail unit with wings of Scheibe SF-27M sailplane

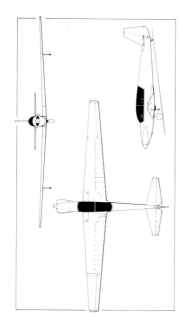

Photo: RF5 (RF4D in background)
Drawing: RF5

Data: RF5

Power plant: One Sportavia-Limbach SL 1700E Comet four-cylinder piston engine (68 hp)

Wing span: 45 ft 1 in (13.74 m)

Length overall: 25 ft 7¼ in (7.80 m)

Weight empty, equipped: 921 lb (418 kg)

STAMPE S.V.4 (Belgium / France)

Data: S.V.4C
Power plant: One Renault 4 Pei four-cylinder piston engine (140 hp)
Wing span: 27 ft 6 in (8.38 m)
Length overall: 22 ft 10 in (6.96 m)
Weight empty: 1 106 lb (502 kg)
Gross weight: 1 720 lb (780 kg)
Max cruising speed at S/L: 95 knots (109 mph; 175 km/h)
Max rate of climb at S/L: approx 1 080 ft (330 m)/min
Service ceiling: 16 400 ft (5 000 m)
Accommodation: Two seats in tandem. Dual controls. Space for 110 lb (50 kg) baggage

Variants:

S.V.4. Initial Belgian (Stampe et Vertongen) version: 120 hp de Havilland Gipsy III engine

S.V.4B. Development of S.V.4: 130 hp Gipsy Major I engine

S.V.4C. French-built (SNCA du Nord) version of S.V.4B: Renault engine, as described above. Production (700) completed

S.V.4D. Belgian (Stampe et Renard) version of S.V.4B/C: 165 hp Rolls-Royce Continental IO-346-A flat-four engine, new main landing gear. Prototype only. Flown 1967

First flight 1933

Primary trainer and club aircraft

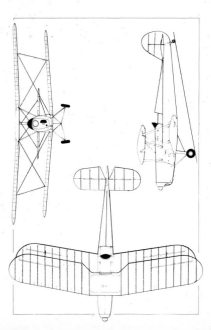

Photo and Drawing: S.V.4C (front cockpit covered)

TED SMITH AEROSTAR series (USA)

First flight 1967

Light transport

Wing span: 34 ft 2½ in (10.43 m)
Length overall: 34 ft 9¾ in (10.61 m)
Cabin:
  Length: 12 ft 6 in (3.81 m)
  Width: 3 ft 10 in (1.17 m)
  Height: 4 ft 0 in (1.22 m)
Baggage space: 30 cu ft (0.85 m³)
Weight empty, equipped: 3 425 lb (1 553 kg)
Max T-O weight: 5 500 lb (2 495 kg)
Cruising speed (70% power) at 10 000 ft (3 050 m): 217 knots (250 mph; 402 km/h)
Rate of climb at S/L: 1 850 ft (564 m)/min
Service ceiling: 22 000 ft (6 705 m)
Range (65% power) at 10 000 ft (3 050 m), with max fuel and 30 min reserve: 1 216 nm (1 400 miles; 2 250 km)
Accommodation: Seating for six persons. Large utility shelf in aft cabin. Baggage compartment, capacity 240 lb (109 kg), aft of cabin. Dual controls standard

Variants:
Model 600. Initial version, as described above. In production
Model 601. As Model 600 but 290 hp Lycoming TIO-540 turbocharged engines. In production
Model 601P. As Model 600 but 300 hp Lycoming TIO-541 turbocharged engines, pressurised cabin. In production
Model 700. Slightly larger than Model 600. 350 hp Lycoming IO-540-M engines. In production
Model 700P. As Model 700 but Lycoming turbocharged engines and pressurised cabin. Under development

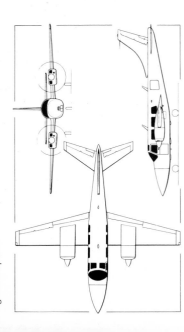

Photo: Model 600
Drawing: Model 601

Data: Model 600
Power plant: Two Lycoming IO-540 six-cylinder piston engines (each 290 hp)

TRANSAVIA PL-12 AIRTRUK (Australia)

First flight 1965

Agricultural and utility aircraft

Data: PL-12-U
Power plant: One Continental IO-520-D six-cylinder piston engine (300 hp)
Wing span: 39 ft 10½ in (12. 15 m)
Length overall: 20 ft 10 in (6. 35 m)
Passenger cabin:
Length: 9 ft 0 in (2.74 m)
Max width: 3 ft 2 in (0.97 m)
Max height: 6 ft 11 in (2.11 m)
Volume 74 cu ft (2.10 m³)
Weight empty: 1 830 lb (830 kg)
Max T-O weight: 3 800 lb (1 723 kg)
Max cruising speed (75% power) at S/L, ISA: 102 knots (117 mph; 118 km/h)
Max rate of climb at S/L: 800 ft (244 m)/min
Service ceiling: 10 500 ft (3 200 m)
Range with max payload: 650 nm (748 miles; 1 203 km)
Range with max fuel: 700 nm (806 miles; 1 297 km)
Accommodation: Single-seat cockpit for pilot. One passenger on upper deck and four more passengers on lower deck. Can also be used as a cargo, ambulance or aerial survey aircraft. In PL-12 agricultural version, the passenger cabin area is occupied mainly by the chemical tank or hopper, but there is a smaller cabin area available aft of this to permit two ground-crew members to be carried
Variants:
PL-12. Standard one/three-seat agricultural version, with 180 Imp gallon (818 litre) chemical tank. In production
PL-12-U. Utility version, as described above. In production

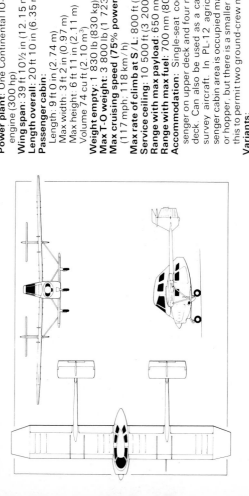

239

Photo: PL-12
Drawing: PL-12-U

First flights 1960/1966

Four-seat general utility aircraft

UTVA-60/66 (Yugoslavia)

Data: UTVA-66
Power plant: One Lycoming GSO-480-B1J6 six-cylinder piston engine (270 hp)
Wing span: 37 ft 5 in (11.40 m)
Length overall: 27 ft 6 in (8.38 m)
Cabin: Length: 4 ft 11 in (1.50 m) Width: 3 ft 5 in (1.05 m), Height: 3ft 11 in (1.20 m)
Weight empty, equipped: 2 756 lb (1 250 kg)
Max T-O weight: 4 000 lb (1 814 kg)
Max cruising speed at optimum height: 124 knots (143 mph; 230 km/h)
Max rate of climb at S/L: 885 ft (270 m)/min
Service ceiling: 22 000 ft (6 700 m)
Range with standard fuel: 404 nm (466 miles; 750 km)
Accommodation: Seating for pilot and three passengers. Ambulance version carries pilot, two stretchers and attendant.

UTVA-66. Development of basic four-seat UTVA-60-AT1. Can be used for glider towing. In production
UTVA-66-AM. Ambulance version. In production
UTVA-66-H. Twin-float version, similar to standard UTVA-66 but with the latter's optional auxiliary fuel tanks fitted as standard. In production

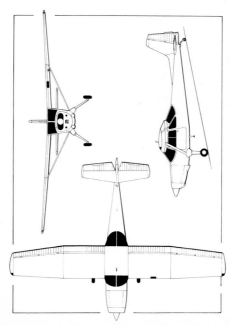

241

Photo and Drawing: UTVA-66

UTVA-65 PRIVREDNIK series (Yugoslavia)

First flight 1965

Agricultural aircraft

Data: Super Privrednik-350

Power plant: One Lycoming IGO-540-A1C six-cylinder piston engine (350 hp)

Wing span: 44 ft 0½ in (13.42 m)

Length overall: 27 ft 9 in (8.46 m)

Payload: 1 455 lb (660 kg)

Max T-O weight (Restricted category, with spraying equipment): 4 409 lb (2 000 kg)

Max level speed (estimated): 121 knots (140 mph; 225 km/h)

Max rate of climb at S/L, full load (estimated): 590 ft (180 m)/min

Accommodation: Single seat. Plastics hopper forward of cockpit

Equipment: Transland application equipment standard. Aircraft can be used for spraying (spraybars or Micronair), dusting or top-dressing

Variants:

Privrednik-GO. Initial version. 295 hp Lycoming GO-480-G1A6 engine, constant-speed propeller

Privrednik-IO. Export version of -GO. Lycoming IO-540-K1A5 engine, choice of fixed-pitch or constant-speed propeller, softer landing gear

Super Privrednik-350. More powerful version, as described above. In production

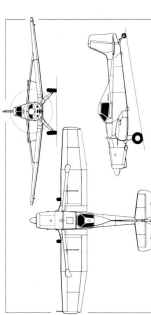

Photo: Super Privrednik-350
Drawing: Privrednik-GO

243

WASSMER WA 51 PACIFIC, WA 52 EUROPA and WA 54 ATLANTIC (France)

First flight 1966

Four-seat light aircraft

Data: WA 51 Pacific

Power plant: One Lycoming O-320-E2A four-cylinder piston engine (150 hp)

Wing span: 30 ft 10 in (9.40 m)

Length overall: 23 ft 11½ in (7.30 m)

Weight empty: 1 320 lb (600 kg)

Max T-O weight: 2 292 lb (1 040 kg)

Max cruising speed at 5 500 ft (1 675 m): 120 knots (138 mph; 222 km/h)

Max rate of climb at S/L: 787 ft (240 m)/min

Service ceiling: 14 450 ft (4 400 m)

Range with max fuel: 490 nm (565 miles; 910 km)

Accommodation: Seating for four persons. Baggage compartment behind rear seats

Variants:

WA 51 Pacific. Basic version, as described above: improved version designated **WA 51A.** In production

WA 52 Europa. Similar to WA 51 but 160 hp engine, optional auxiliary fuel tank. In production

WA 54 Atlantic. Similar to WA 51 but 180 hp Lycoming O-360 engine, extra baggage space, landing gear and other improvements. In production

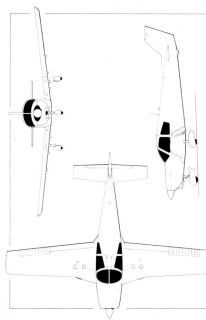

Photo: WA 54 Atlantic
Drawing: WA 51A Pacific

245

WSK-OKECIE PZL-101A GAWRON (ROOK) (Poland)

First flight 1958

Agricultural, ambulance and utility aircraft

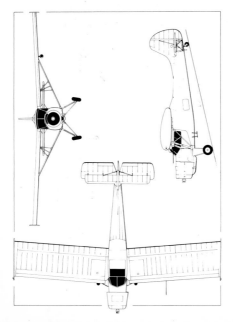

Wing span:
endplate wingtips: 41 ft 7½ in (12.68 m)
laminar-flow wingtips: 42 ft 9 in (13.03 m)
Length overall: 29 ft 6½ in (9.00 m)
Cabin volume: 90 cu ft (2.55 m³)
Weight empty, equipped:
agricultural: 2 260 lb (1 025 kg)
ambulance: 2 354 lb (1 068 kg)
Max T-O weight: 3 660 lb (1 660 kg)
Max cruising speed (agricultural version): 70 knots (81 mph; 130 km/h)
Max rate of climb at S/L (agricultural version): 530 ft (162 m)/min
Service ceiling (agricultural version): 11 100 ft (3 380 m)
Range with max internal fuel (agricultural version): 356 nm (410 miles; 660 km)
Range with external tanks (agricultural version): 614 nm (708 miles; 1 140 km)

Accommodation and equipment: Standard agricultural version has seating for pilot and mechanic or loader. The glassfibre hopper has a dustproof hatch and can carry 1 100 lb (500 kg) of dust and a distributor, or 175 Imp gallons (800 litres) of liquid chemical and spraybars. Pilot and either two stretcher patients and attendant (ambulance) or three passengers (utility version). Dual controls optional. With passenger seats removed, utility model can carry 660 lb (300 kg) of cargo

Variants: Three basic versions (agricultural, ambulance and utility), with equipment according to role; all are designated PZL-101A. Late-production aircraft have laminar-flow wingtips instead of the original type fitted with endplates

Power plant: One Ivchenko AI-14R nine-cylinder radial piston engine (260 hp)

247

WSK-OKECIE PZL-104 WILGA (THRUSH) (Poland)

Light general-purpose aircraft

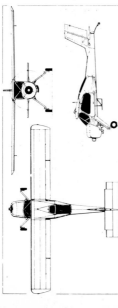

Photo and Drawing: Wilga 35

Data: Wilga 35

Power plant: One Ivchenko AI-14R nine-cylinder radial piston engine (260 hp)

Wing span: 36 ft 4⅞ in (11.14 m)

Length overall: 26 ft 6¾ in (8.10 m)

Cabin: Length: 7 ft 2½ in (2.20 m)

Max width: 3 ft 10 in (1.20 m), Height: 4 ft 11 in (1.50 m)

Weight empty, equipped: 1874 lb (850 kg)

Max T-O weight: 2755 lb (1250 kg)

Max cruising speed: 104 knots (120 mph; 193 km/h)

Max rate of climb at S/L: 1245 ft (380 m)/min

Service ceiling: 15025 ft (4580 m)

Range (max fuel, 30 min res): 366 nm (422 miles; 680 km)

Accommodation: Passenger version accommodates four persons, including pilot. Baggage compartment aft of seats. A controllable towing hook can be attached to tow a glider of up to 1433 lb (650 kg) weight or two or three gliders with combined weight of 2480 lb (1125 kg)

Variants: Wilga 1, prototype. **Wilga 2**, redesigned prototype (Wilga 2P four seat, Wilga 2R after conversion to agricultural role). **Wilga C**, prototype for export version. **Wilga 3P**, initial production four-seat/liaison. **Wilga CP**, as 3P, with engine change; built in Poland and (as the **Gelatik**) Indonesia. **Wilga 3A**, fitted for club flying, parachuting, glider towing. **Wilga CA**, as 3A but with engine change. **Wilga 3C**, as CP, with new tailplane, tailwheel and forward inclined landing gear legs. **Wilga 3D**, dual control version of 3P. **Wilga CD**, as 3D with engine change. **Wilga 3R**, agricultural version of 3P. **Wilga CR**, as 3R with engine change. **Wilga 3S**, ambulance version of 3P. **Wilga CS**, as 3S, with engine change. **Wilga 32**, improved version from 1967. In production in Poland, in Aeroclub (32A), Passenger (32P), ambulance (32S) versions; and in Indonesia as Gelatik 32. **Wilga 35**, same improvements as 32, but retaining AL-14R engine. Current versions Wilga 35A, 35P, 35S. **Wilga 40**, experimental version (1969) with automatic leading-edge slats, all-moving tailplane and detachable cargo or fuel pack. **Wilga 43**, experimental version similar to Wilga 40 but with engine change

YAKOVLEV Yak-18 (USSR)

First flight 1946

NATO code name *Max*

Single- or two-seat training and aerobatic aircraft

Length overall: 27 ft 4¾ in (8.35 m)
Max T-O weight: 2 425 lb (1 100 kg)
Max level speed: 173 knots (199 mph; 320 km/h)
Max rate of climb at S/L: 1 970 ft (600 m)/min
Range with max fuel: 217 nm (250 miles; 400 km)
Accommodation: Single seat

Variants:

Yak-18. Initial tandem two-seat version: 160 hp M-11FR engine in "helmeted" cowling, tailwheel landing gear

Yak-18U. Modified Yak-18: tricycle landing gear (main units of which retract forward), lengthened front fuselage

Yak-18A. Development of Yak-18U: 260 hp AI-14R (later 300 hp AI-14RF) engine, NACA-type cowling, enlarged cockpit canopy, dorsal fin extension

Yak-18P. Single-seat development of Yak-18A for advanced training, including aerobatics. Built in two versions: one with cockpit aft of wing and forward-retracting main wheels, the other with cockpit over wing and inward-retracting main wheels. Fuel system for 5 min inverted flying. Longer-span ailerons

Yak-18PM. Single-seat aerobatic version, as described above, produced for 1966 World Aerobatic Championships: AI-14RF engine, reduced dihedral, cockpit further aft than on Yak-18P

Yak-18PS. Similar to Yak-18PM, but tailwheel landing gear

Yak-18T. Extensively-redesigned version, first revealed 1967. Entirely new fuselage, four-seat cabin, increased-span wings with squarer tips, enlarged rudder, retractable tricycle landing gear, 300 hp AI-14RF engine

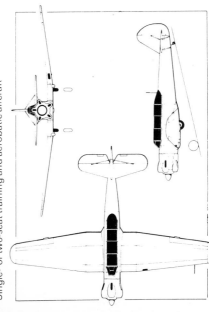

Photo: Yak-18PM
Drawing: Yak-18

Data: Yak-18PM
Power plant: One Ivchenko AI-14RF nine-cylinder radial piston engine (300 hp)
Wing span: 34 ft 9¼ in (10.60 m)

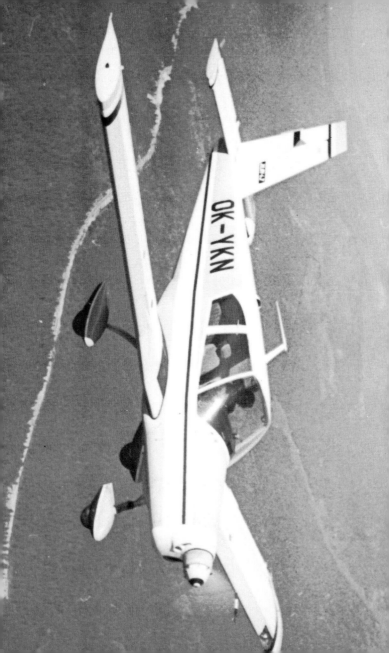

ZLIN 42 / 43 (Czechoslovakia)

First flights 1967/1968

Two- or four-seat light aircraft

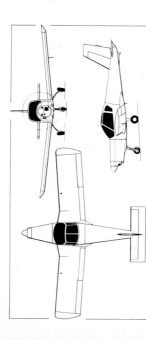

Photo: Zlin 43
Drawing: Zlin 42

Data: Zlin 43
Power plant: One Avia M 337 six-cylinder piston engine (210 hp)
Wing span: 32 ft 0¼ in (9.76 m)
Length overall: 25 ft 5 in (7.75 m)

Cabin:
Length: 8 ft 2½ in (2.50 m)
Width: 3 ft 8 in (1.12 m)
Height: 3 ft 11¼ in (1.20 m)
Baggage space (inside cabin): 7.1 cu ft (0.2 m³)
Baggage compartment (rear): 8.8 cu ft (0.25 m³)
Basic weight, equipped: 1 609 lb (730 kg)
Max T-O weight:
Normal: 2 976 lb (1 350 kg)
Utility: 2 204 lb (1 000 kg)
Max cruising speed: 113 knots (130 mph; 210 km/h)
Max rate of climb at S/L: 689 ft (210 m)/min
Service ceiling: 12 465 ft (3 800 m)
Max range (standard fuel): 325 nm (375 miles; 610 km)
Max range (with wingtip tanks): 590 nm (680 miles; 1 100 km)

Accommodation: Seating for up to four persons. Baggage space behind rear bench seat. Additional baggage compartment in rear of fuselage. Dual controls optional

Variants:
Zlin 42. Two-seater: 180 hp Avia M 137 A engine, dual controls standard. In production
Zlin 43. Four-seater, as described above. Substantially similar to Zlin 42, but slightly larger overall and with more powerful engine. Enlarged centre-fuselage to accommodate four-seat cabin; inboard wing leading-edges swept forward. In production

ZLIN TRENER series (Czechoslovakia)

First flight 1947

Two-seat training and aerobatic light aircraft

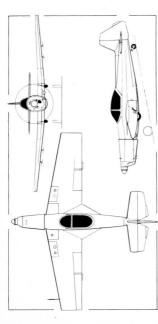

Photo: Zlin 326 Trener-Master
Drawing: Zlin 526 AFS

Data: Zlin 526 F Trener
Power plant: One Avia M 137 A six-cylinder engine (180 hp)
Wing span: 34 ft 9 in (10.60 m)
Wing span over tip-tanks: 35 ft 11 ½ in (10.96 m)
Length overall: 26 ft 3 in (8.00 m)
Weight empty: 1 465 lb (665 kg)
Max T-O weight:
Aerobatic: 2 072 lb (940 kg), Normal: 2 150 lb (975 kg)
Max cruising speed at max Normal T-O weight: 113 knots (130 mph; 210 km/h)

Rate of climb at S/L, above weight: 1 181 ft (360 m/min)
Service ceiling, weight as above: 17 060 ft (5 200 m)
Max range with standard fuel, weight as above: 255 nm (295 miles; 480 km)
Max range with wingtip tanks, weight as above: 450 nm (520 miles; 840 km)
Accommodation: Seating for two in tandem. Dual controls
Equipment: Optional equipment for glider-towing
Variants:

Zlin 26 Trener. Initial wooden-construction version
Zlin 126 Trener. Metal-construction version of Zlin 26
Zlin 226A Akrobat and 226AS Akrobat Special. Fully aerobatic single-seat versions of Zlin 226T
Zlin 226B Bohatyr. Glider-towing version of Zlin 226T
Zlin 226T Trener-6. Development of Zlin 126
Zlin 526 Trener-Master. Development of Zlin 326: constant-speed propeller, crew positions reversed (pilot at rear)
Zlin 326A Akrobat. Fully-aerobatic version of Zlin 326
Zlin 526 Trener-Master. Development of Zlin 326: constant-speed propeller, pilot at rear
Zlin 526A Akrobat and 526AS Akrobat Special. Fully-aerobatic versions of 526; 526AS one-piece canopy
Zlin 526 F Trener. Development of Zlin 526. In production
Zlin 526 L Trener. Similar to Zlin 526 F but 200 hp Lycoming AIO-360-B1B engine. In production
Zlin 526 AFS Akrobat. Single-seat version of Zlin 526 F for advanced aerobatics. In production
Zlin 726 Universal. Similar to Zlin 526 F but 180 hp M 137 AZ engine, shorter-span wings, etc. In production

INDEX

INDEX